# *Thematic Inquiry*

# *through Fiction*

# *and Nonfiction*

## *PreK to Grade 6*

## Colleen MacDonell

Linworth Books

Linworth Publishing, Inc.
Columbus, Ohio

Trademarks: Rather than put a trademark symbol with every occurrence of a trademarked name, we note that we are using the names simply in an editorial fashion and to the benefit of the trademark owner, with no intention of infringement of the trademark.

Library of Congress Cataloging-in-Publication Data

MacDonell, Colleen.
 Thematic inquiry through fiction and nonfiction, PreK to grade 6 / Colleen MacDonell.
   p. cm.
 Includes bibliographical references and index.
 ISBN-13: 978-1-58683-350-3 (pbk.)
 ISBN-10: 1-58683-350-2 (pbk.)
 1. Inquiry-based learning. 2. Education, Elementary--Curricula. 3. Active learning. I. Title.
 LB1027.44.M325 2009
 372.19--dc22

                    2008033365


Cynthia Anderson: Editor
Judi Repman: Consulting Editor

Published by Linworth Publishing, Inc.
3650 Olentangy River Road
Suite 250
Columbus, Ohio 43214

ISBN 13: 978-1-58683-350-3
ISBN 10: 1-58683-350-2

5 4 3 2

**Mixed Sources**
Product group from well-managed
forests and other controlled sources
www.fsc.org  Cert no. SW-COC-002283
© 1996 Forest Stewardship Council
FSC

# Table of Contents

# Table of Contents (continued)

# Table of Contents *(continued)*

# Table of Contents *(continued)*

# *Table of Contents* (continued)

# Table of Contents *(continued)*

# Table of Figures

# Acknowledgments

Thanks to my husband, Dominic Larkin, for his patience and encouragement.

# About the Author

 Colleen MacDonell is the Library Coordinator of three libraries at a PreK to Grade 12 school. She holds a B.A. and M.A. in English Literature, plus an education diploma and M.L.I.S. She has taught college courses on a wide variety of library science topics, including children's literature and school libraries. Colleen is a frequent presenter at international library conferences and educational workshops. She is a past Director for International Schools for IASL. This is her third book.

# Preface

For many years I have worked in schools that embrace and support the inquiry approach to learning. This book is the result of my own inquiry into what I do every day as a library media specialist.

While still new to inquiry-based learning I read for background knowledge, asked a lot of questions, made observations of colleagues and students, attended conferences related to the subject, and shared ideas online. As my knowledge and experience grew, I began to formulate new questions and test new ideas. I read widely to answer questions. I presented at conferences and benefited from the feedback of other teachers and librarians. I gave myself lots of time along the way for reflection and thought.

This process has been a lengthy and personal attempt to clarify concepts at a metacognitive level. Because the questions are complex and come from real-life experience and needs, the process never ends. Understanding inquiry is truly a lifelong learning goal for an educator. However, at some point in the process, an inquirer is ready to share what they know—their newly constructed understandings—with an audience asking the same kinds of questions. This book represents what I have learned about inquiry through all the successes and failures that come with the daily practice of helping children make meaning from experience.

# Introduction

This book shows librarians and teachers alike how inquiry-based learning can happen if we ask good questions, provide good resources, and properly facilitate the learning process. Teachers know that inquiry is a motivating, student-centered approach to learning. However, many feel they cannot use an inquiry approach to learning and still cover their core curriculum content. This book models how the inquiry process can work with typical core curriculum in key subject areas. It is possible to adopt this innovative and worthwhile pedagogical method and still achieve curriculum standards.

Chapter 1 introduces the concept of inquiry-based learning and answers some questions: How did this approach develop? How does inquiry work in practice? What is the role of the teacher and the librarian during a unit of inquiry? How can the principal support inquiry? How do we keep children motivated throughout the process? This chapter provides evidence of the benefits to both students and educators who use inquiry to cover core content. A handout defining inquiry concludes this chapter.

Chapter 2 looks at how inquiry works in practice. Questions are at the heart of inquiry. How do we ensure that inquiry is guided by good questions? How do we differentiate between questions? What questions are most appropriate for resource-based inquiry? How can we ensure that questions can be addressed using resources? This chapter shows how good guiding questions are developed, then how these questions are refined or broken down for further investigation using stories and informational resources. This chapter is essential reading before broaching the units that follow. Handouts for inquiry units conclude the chapter: for thinking about questions with students, finding your way during resource-based inquiry, reflecting on the inquiry process, and helping older students keep themselves organized as inquiry gets under way.

Chapters 3 through 6 outline specific units of inquiry. Each unit begins by determining the feasibility of the topic. "A Good Choice for Inquiry" examines whether there are age-appropriate resources available to ensure success, why the topic itself is likely to be motivating for children, and how the topic can be made relevant to the lives and local community of the students. This is the crucial test of an inquiry theme.

Next, statements from national education standards in the United States that fit the unit of inquiry are identified. Only the primary focus of the content is addressed. For example, in the study of pests in our environment, the focus is science and social studies. Even though language and math skills would be called upon, these learning goals are not listed. Guiding Questions are developed to focus an inquiry unit by grade levels: PreK to K, Grades 1 to 2, Grades 3 to 4, and Grades 5 to 6. Each unit looks at resources that can be used to generate interest and creative thinking about a topic of inquiry and then continues with resources that address specific questions. Specific questions that can be answered with resources are Resource-Ready Questions. They differ fundamentally from the Guiding Questions, or questions better suited to hands-on experimentation or seeking expert opinion. An important part of the inquiry process is helping children break down guiding questions into those questions that require hands-on work with the teacher, those that could be answered by a local expert, and those that can be answered through print and multimedia resources in the library. Strategies vary by grade level and type of resource.

Topics are chosen that fit with core curricula because they are deemed to be important for children—and indeed for adults—to know. Whether children consider them important depends on the extent to which educators can engage their imaginations and intellects. An inquiry approach to learning can make the topic relevant to children because it begins with questions about their own world and experience and thoughts. Ultimately, the goal of inquiry is to make children think about their behavior and act in an informed, intelligent way. It is the first step on a journey of lifelong learning about how we as responsible persons and citizens choose to act.

This book covers the resources to support inquiry—identifies them and tells how to use them. It does not describe the whole process—the classroom activities, discussions, field trips, guest speakers, experiments, observations, or interviews that are a necessary part of the process. These hands-on activities will vary from school to school, depending on the availability of local experts, the local flora and fauna, opportunities for field trips. However, from time to time a boxed text gives readers a suggestion or nudge in a direction that might appeal to the particular students and circumstances of their school.

Resources are chosen based on age-appropriateness, with some consideration given to English Language Learners (ELL) or special needs students. Didactic, unimaginative books that preach rather than guide do not appear in these pages. High priority has been given to resources that will first astound and inspire children and then answer their serious desire for knowledge with clear and well-presented information. Highly interactive resources (especially those online) are favored. The resources are chosen to address all student questions on each inquiry unit. Resource-Ready Collections are mean to address specific questions that are developed from the Guiding Questions. These lists are presented as a core collection (those resources that are considered absolutely necessary for the unit) and supplementary collection (resources that repeat topics or address items of particular, local interest).

Read through the entire introduction and chapters 1 and 2. They are important background to understanding the rest of the book. The chapters that follow—chapters 3 through 6—can be browsed depending on which topics, curriculum level, or grade level is most of interest to you. The book concludes with a works cited list.

These units of inquiry are ready to use. All the library media specialist needs to do is collect the resources and interest a teacher in collaborating. Making use of the Guiding Questions to focus the inquiry ensures that students make it to the end with a relevant and interesting product. What that product finally looks like depends not on the resources that have been used as much as the individual students and teachers and their unique take on how to creatively interpret the information into a knowledge product.

These units can serve as a model for teachers, library media specialists, parents, or administrators who want to see how their school can embrace inquiry. It demonstrates how to take the content of a prescribed curriculum and transform it into a rewarding, student-centered learning experience. For anyone who believes that inquiry can and should be done in schools—this book shows you how to do it!

# Chapter 1

# Setting the Stage for Inquiry-Based Learning

*"Dewey advocated learning by doing, and a curriculum that involved the mind, hands, and heart."*

—Partnership for 21st Century Skills

## Understanding Inquiry

Before planning collaborative units of inquiry, it is important that teachers, librarians, and administrators understand inquiry: how inquiry is defined; what attitudes and beliefs are conducive to inquiry; how inquiry fits within the curriculum; models of inquiry; and how a culture of inquiry can benefit children, parents, teachers, and the school as a whole. Every answer must be framed to address the needs of young children as they move through the early childhood and elementary school years.

Implementing inquiry may require structural changes within a school, such as a shift from fixed to flexible scheduling in the library or setting aside time for collaborative planning. More importantly, according to Diane Oberg, is the need to re-examine the educational norms of the school and individual teachers. Learning about inquiry necessarily affects currently held educational beliefs and practices, leading to what Oberg calls "teacher transformation" (31). As educators read, discuss, and implement inquiry, they reflect on how well their educational philosophy and classroom practice fit with this approach. In fact, they participate in the very process that they are implementing: an inquiry into how they teach and how children learn.

### Hands-On Learning

Inquiry is often prefaced by the term "hands-on." This experiential approach to learning had a vocal and influential advocate in John Dewey. As early as 1902, he called for "personal contact and immediate individual experience" of the concept or phenomena being studied *(The Child and the Curriculum 20)*. Pine and Aschbacher follow this line of thinking all the way back to the 17th century.

What are these inquiry curricula, and what was their genesis? Beginning at least in the 17th century when Galileo rolled balls down ramps, scientific research has been based on inquiry—experimental investigations that attempt to answer questions about the natural world.

Science curricula in America have been focused on inquiry since 1960, first with the NSF-funded inquiry-based Physical Science Study Committee (PSSC) and later with the Elementary Science Study (ESS), Science Curriculum Improvement Study (SCIS), and Science—A Process Approach (SAPA) (Pine and Aschbacher). Many excellent definitions and guidelines for inquiry come from science educators. For instance, an inquiry approach called the learning cycle grew out of the Science Curriculum Improvement Study. Students "learn through their own involvement and action . . . .The goal is to allow students to apply previous knowledge, develop interests, and initiate and maintain a curiosity toward the materials at hand" (Trowbridge and Bybee 306). While this is a good description, it may lead some to believe that inquiry is only amenable to learning science.

Phillip J. Vanfossen and James Shiveley argue that "inquiry-oriented teaching might be the most appropriate methodology for the social studies, regardless of grade level." Quoting Dewey, they note that inquiry nurtures a child's "natural tendency to investigate" and "develops many of the essential skills and dispositions associated with democratic citizenship" (an explicit goal of the National Council for the Social Studies). Karen Short, Jerome Harste, and Carolyn Burke take an inquiry approach to reading and writing that, as Daniel Callison notes, has been used in many curricular areas (Callison 62). Jeff Wilhelm, founder of the Boise State Writing Project, advocates the use of inquiry for any subject within the elementary school curriculum—from language to science to math.

# Minds-On Learning

True inquiry is not only "hands-on" but "minds-on" (Van Tassell 42). Children can be asked to do hands-on activities all day long. Whether they are engaged or not depends on how personally meaningful the task is to them. Students might spend a day doing experiments, playing tennis, making clay sculptures, brainstorming questions, writing thought webs, writing reflections, listening to music, and thinking of how to solve a problem. This seems like a very full day indeed, but it could, in fact, be two very different days—a day of going through the motions to please a teacher or a day of actively participating in real learning.

# Hearts-On Learning

Complete personal involvement is necessary to inquiry. Children who care about a topic will ask better questions, be more creative in problem-solving, and persist when difficulties arise. It is no accident that these are precisely the skills and attitudes that are associated with success in work and in life. Alfie Kohn asks us to think about our own working lives: ". . . just as adults who love their work will invariably do a better job than those goaded with artificial incentives, so children are more likely to be optimal learners if they are interested in what they are learning" (144). Thus, one of the questions that teachers should ask themselves and their students before beginning inquiry is: "Do we really care about this question?" Figure 1.1 Defining Inquiry presents a quick overview of what inquiry is—and is not.

Figure 1.1  Defining Inquiry

# Inquiry Is…

- ☐ Being motivated to learn
- ☐ Asking questions that are important
- ☐ Being comfortable not knowing
- ☐ Being persistent
- ☐ Seeing mistakes as opportunities
- ☐ Recognizing the strengths of others
- ☐ Knowing what a good question is
- ☐ Central to lifelong learning
- ☐ Working with purpose
- ☐ Seeing the connection between school and real life
- ☐ Trans-disciplinary
- ☐ Collaborative
- ☐ Suited to any subject
- ☐ Something we get better at the more we do
- ☐ Fun for everyone
- ☐ A learning experience for everyone

# Inquiry Is Not…

- ☐ Just about science
- ☐ Just asking questions
- ☐ Something outside of the curriculum
- ☐ Just done in school
- ☐ Boring
- ☐ Just for high achievers
- ☐ About pleasing the teacher
- ☐ Finding facts
- ☐ Reporting on a theme
- ☐ Predictable
- ☐ Chaotic
- ☐ About right and wrong answers
- ☐ Time consuming
- ☐ Teacher-centered
- ☐ Difficult to do

# Models of Inquiry

Callison and Leslie Preddy believe inquiry gets better the more children do it. They encourage teachers to do inquiry in a controlled or directed manner if the children are inexperienced inquirers. In this case, inquiry grows out of stimulating questions pre-selected from the curriculum for their high interest appeal and feasibility. With experience, children can take part in guided inquiry that uses as many of their own questions as possible. Once children are experienced inquirers, they will naturally take inquiry out of the classroom and incorporate it into their own lives. This final stage will evince the three independent learning standards defined by Information Power (23-32).

Carol Kuhlthau and Ross Todd describe guided inquiry as "carefully planned, closely supervised targeted intervention of an instructional team of school librarians and teachers." Whatever their level of experience, teachers and students need a model to guide them through the inquiry process. For Jean Donham, a model provides a "common lexicon" that ensures teaching professionals understand one another (22). Once a unit of inquiry is begun, the model helps remind teachers about the kinds of intervention that may be required at each stage of inquiry. Students benefit from consistent use of just one model because it gives them plenty of time to internalize inquiry as a process.

There are many, many models of inquiry in use today—from simple to complex. Among the most popular models of inquiry in school libraries are the Big6™, Pathways to Knowledge®, and the Information Search Process (ISP). Other schools, districts, or governments develop their own models, as with the InfoZone model and Alberta Inquiry Model, both developed in Canada. Most models can be viewed on the Internet (see "Inquiry Models on the Internet" for further examples).

Whatever model is finally chosen by a school or district, Donham suggests changing educational jargon or complex wording into kid-friendly language before presenting it to children (22). A simplified model gives children a touchstone to mark their progress. As they focus on particular tasks they begin to internalize the process of inquiry. This internalization of the process is a necessary preparation for the metacognitive task of reflection on the process itself.

Very young children need a special model with no more than three steps. The Project Approach is a simple, three-step model that is widely used (Helm and Katz 9). The Super3™ is a simplified version of the Big6™ that Eisenberg and Berkowitz developed after requests from teachers in the preschool and lower elementary years. Kuhlthau believes "there is a need to accommodate inquiry tasks to the child's level of cognitive ability" (4). For children "in pre-kindergarten through fifth grade," this involves three actions: asking questions, finding answers, and sharing new knowledge (4).

All of these models and many more are variations on a theme. Almost all, as Callison notes, include these essential elements: questioning, exploration, assimilation, inference, and reflection (Callison and Preddy 51). Educators can choose to follow the model that makes most sense to them. From the perspective of the library media specialist, the important part of the process focuses on the answering of resource-ready questions. Chapter 2 will look in detail at how questions are developed and refined for successful use of resources and some of the roles that can clarify how resources are used within an inquiry model.

# Inquiry Models on the Internet

**The Big6™**
<http://www.big6.com>
*An information problem-solving approach developed by Michael B. Eisenberg and Robert E. Berkowitz*

**The Super3™**
<http://www.big6.com/kids/K-2.htm>
*A model for very young children developed by Michael B. Eisenberg and Robert E. Berkowitz*

**Pathways to Knowledge®**
<http://www.sparkfactor.com/clients/follett/home.html>
*A model that applies inquiry to information literacy, sponsored by Follett and developed by Marjorie L. Pappas and Ann E. Tepe*

**Inquiry Page™**
<https://apps.lis.uiuc.edu/wiki/display/fa06lis590ibo/Inquiry+project>
*Developed by Bertram C. Bruce and the Inquiry Project at the University of Illinois at Urbana-Champaign*

**Information Search Process (ISP)©**
<http://www.scils.rutgers.edu/~kuhlthau/information_search_process.htm>
*Developed by Kuhlthau and based on her own research*

**The 8Ws ©**
<http://virtualinquiry.com/inquiry/topic72model.pdf>
*Developed by Annette Lamb*

**FLIP it!™**
<http://www.aliceinfo.org/flipit/>
*Developed for student researchers by Alice Yucht*

**The Research Cycle ©**
<http://questioning.org/rcycle.html>
*Developed by Jamie McKenzie*

**The Project Approach ©**
<http://www.projectapproach.org>
*Developed by Judy Harris Helm and Lillian Katz*

**InfoZone ©**
<http://www.pembinatrails.ca/infozone>
*Developed by the Pembina Trails School Division (Manitoba, Canada)*

**Alberta Inquiry Model ©**
<http://www.education.gov.ab.ca/K_12/curriculum/bysubject/focusoninquiry.pdf>
*Guidelines and a model of inquiry developed by the government of Albert, Canada*

# Implementing Inquiry-Based Learned

## Inquiry and Teachers

Most teachers, even unsuspectingly, have used inquiry-based learning. Inquiry may happen informally and unintentionally, as students raise questions that were not anticipated by the teacher. This kind of learning is called "authentic curriculum" because it grows out of the student's own desire for knowledge. While teachers recognize the value of such questions, this authentic curriculum is often seen as a diversion from the prescribed curriculum set forth by one's department of education or school board. Once the unplanned-for discussion has taken place, the class returns to the "real" content of the lesson and the transmission of knowledge from teacher to pupil.

For others, inquiry happens only in particular subject areas or during special kinds of activities. Asking students to predict what will happen during a scientific experiment or to note observations and questions during a field trip are viewed as inquiry-based learning. Core content that has a strong hands-on and practical aspect (as with much science content) is more obviously amenable to inquiry-based approaches, and thus inquiry is not seen as a diversion from the curriculum for teachers when they are doing science. Teachers often have a higher comfort level with inquiry in the science curriculum than social studies or language studies.

Finally, there are teachers who take the view that learning is inquiry. Rather than see it as an extra or a luxury that might be squeezed in between content-driven lessons, inquiry is adopted as an approach to learning content—whether prescribed or not. This requires a leap of faith for those who have never taught without a textbook or who feel pressured to "cover content." As library media specialists are well aware, this third, more adventurous teacher is an ideal candidate for collaborative planning and resource-based inquiry.

This third category of educators shares a conviction that we learn best by doing. They are constructivists, who "view learning as an active, engaging process in which all aspects of experience are called into play" (Kuhlthau 2). The National Research Council describes even very young children as necessarily active participants in their own learning (58). Children are hard-wired for learning, but they need hands-on experience through exploration and play to make sense of the world. This interaction with the environment helps children to develop their ideas about the world, which Piaget termed "adaptation" (Driscoll and Nagel 68). A constructivist approach to learning is a student-centered practice that assists the child in constructing knowledge rather than passively receiving knowledge directly from the teacher (the transmission approach).

## Inquiry and the Library Program

This understanding of how children learn has profound implications for how we teach and work within school libraries. Kuhlthau sees constructivist theory as a basis "for restructuring the library media center program in order to meet the challenges of the information-age school" (2). Teaching specific library skills or asking children to "repackage" information—even in their own words—is not inquiry.

Library programs need to become integrated with the creative processes of inquiry, where students use information to further true learning. Oberg describes the stages that brought one library media specialist in the Library Power initiative from a "never-in-my-lifetime" attitude to a "personal watershed" and then finally to a leadership role in implementing inquiry-based learning at her school (36-7). This dramatic transformation took place as a result of "inquiry, reflection, and practice"—learning about inquiry, asking questions, using inquiry with students, and thinking about what happened throughout the process (37).

## Principal Support for Inquiry

No matter where teachers and librarians are in their current understanding of inquiry, they need support. The transformational process must allow educators time to reflect on their practice, define professional development needs, participate in meaningful growth through workshops and other staff development activities, and collaborate on new inquiry-based initiatives (Oberg 31). Support comes from the principal who coordinates the implementation and assessment of inquiry-based learning in the school and earmarks the necessary resources: release time for teachers, professional tools, expert trainers or consultants, and increased spending on learning resources for both classroom and library. Donham sees the need for principal support as one of the key lessons learned from the Library Power initiative on inquiry-based learning (30).

# *Inquiry and Learning Standards*

Educators throughout the United States, Canada, the United Kingdom, and Australia have all faced a movement towards accountability in education that has meant a return to core skills (with special emphasis on literacy and numeracy) and a defining of core curriculum content or "essential knowledge." It is beyond the scope of this book to lament or praise this development. It is simply taken as a given. The argument this book does make is that inquiry can still happen, even under the strictures of outcomes-based curricula. In fact, as Leslie Preddy points out, inquiry is a good way to meet standards.

Inquiry is a component of school curriculum, national goals and standards, and many states' standards. It is not something to teach in addition to everything else but rather a method to gain perspective and focus energy while meeting those standards (Callison and Preddy 225).

It is a common misconception that literacy and numeracy skills are not being addressed if you are doing "something else" called inquiry. Olaf Jorgenson and Rick Vanosdall review case after case where studies have shown that inquiry learning improves basic skills performance. After four years of inquiry-based instruction, one group of fourth- and sixth-graders scored approximately 35 percent better in math and 28 percent better in reading, on average, than their classmates who had not been exposed to inquiry-based instruction.

Dewey, in his classic work The School and Society, presciently commented on the fact that subject-specific skills are better taught in the context of inquiry or real life studies than separately as subject disciplines.

> Experience has its geographical aspect, its artistic and its literary, its scientific and its historical sides. All studies arise from aspects of the one earth and the one life lived upon it. We do not have a series of stratified earths, one of which is mathematical, another physical, another historical, and so on. We should not be able to live very long in any one taken by itself. We live in a world where all sides are bound together. All studies grow out of relations in the one great common world. When the child lives in varied but concrete and active relationship to this common world, his studies are naturally unified. It will no longer be a problem to correlate studies. The teacher will not have to resort to all sorts of devices to weave a little arithmetic into the history lesson, and the like. Relate the school to life, and all studies are of necessity correlated. (91)

Even with the constraints of an outcomes-based curriculum, teachers must resist the temptation to return to outmoded educational practices that focus on getting children to pass tests and instead remain true to the vision of children as active participants at the beginning of a journey of lifelong learning. An inquiry approach to learning is a constructivist approach to learning. Using it in the classroom and library media center will ensure that students cover the curriculum and learn in a meaningful and productive way.

Government educational initiatives come and go, but the core curricular needs recommended by subject specialists for the 21st century are widely agreed upon. This book looks to associations of subject-area specialists for guidance on age-appropriate, meaningful topics for inquiry-based learning. Skills and attitudes from information literacy standards that will support inquiry-based learning are taken from the American Association of School Librarians' Standards for the 21st-Century Learner.

# Benefits of Inquiry

Inquiry is an approach that assumes we are teaching for understanding and long-term knowledge rather than short-term memorized facts (Wilhelm). Inquiry builds thinking skills that ensure our students are prepared for the creative workplace of the 21st century rather than the factory of the 19th (Sternberg; Serafini). Children engaged in inquiry learning experience the self-satisfaction that comes "after figuring out a problem" (Uno). Children find meaning. Children experience a process that is memorable. They learn that thinking and investigating is more engaging and worthwhile than cutting and pasting or repeating what a teacher has taught you. The benefits of inquiry are too great to allow passing trends to limit our use of inquiry in the classroom. Because ultimately, real learning is fun.

# Chapter 2

# *Doing Inquiry*

*"Inquiry is a philosophical stance..."*
— Heidi Mills, Curriculum and Development Specialist at the Center for Inquiry

Observe highly effective teachers at work with children and certain common characteristics are sure to emerge. These teachers are keen observers of each individual child in their care. They are fascinated by the way children grow and learn. They take children's ideas and interests seriously, encouraging children to talk and express themselves through art, drama, and play. They listen carefully to what children have to say. They recognize the importance of free play and hands-on exploration, and they take note of children's preoccupations so that they can adapt their own learning goals to the native interests of the child. They motivate children to learn by broaching topics and experiences that are meaningful and interesting to the children. They believe that all children are naturally curious and eager to learn about their world but that they need support to assimilate new knowledge.

These teachers are primed to do inquiry because they already embrace its necessary features. "Inquiry," says Heidi Mills, "is a philosophical stance rather than a set of strategies, activities, or a particular teaching method" (xviii). This approach to learning requires more than just theoretical training and practice. At the most fundamental level, teachers must have a philosophy of teaching that makes inquiry possible.

Our vision as educators guides our daily practice, as Gordon Wells explains (16). Teachers, like students, bring the whole of themselves to their interactions in the classroom; whether they are aware of it or not, their manner of teaching depends not only on what they know but on who they have become (Wells 176).

Teachers who participate in inquiry-based learning are aware of the importance of their personal beliefs about education. One teacher in the Library Power project, an extensive national project involving more than 700 schools, recognized that the real changes required by this approach "were deeper than the things, the materials. They were changes in teaching philosophy..." (Oberg 38). Michele Shamlin believes she was taken on as a teacher in the Center for Inquiry initiative because her "implicit beliefs reflected fundamental features of an inquiry-based model" (55). Doing inquiry obliges us to reflect upon and articulate our philosophy of learning in the context of daily practice. Use Figure 2.1 Reflection Points for Educators Doing Inquiry as a touchstone throughout the inquiry process.

# Resource-Based Inquiry

Many teachers and librarians use the term research to describe the process of finding and using information in text and multimedia formats: "library research" if it takes place in the library; "student research" or "independent research" if it takes place in the classroom or at home. Even the inquiry model may use the term research, and this can create confusion during a collaborative unit.

Inquiry-based learning often incorporates hands-on gathering of data by means of interviews, surveys, or experimentation. For example, children might discover that half of their class takes the bus to school, that each week 40 bags of paper are taken from the school for recycling, or that it is easier to lift a heavy object with a pulley than without. These inquiry activities inform children and lead to the creation of new knowledge. They are, in fact, a simplified version of what researchers mean by the word research.

It is helpful, in the wider context of a thematic inquiry unit, to make a distinction between hands-on research and information seeking. Callison uses the term "information inquiry" to describe "the processes of engaging with text and other media to analyze, extract, synthesize, and infer information that will address student questions" (Callison and Preddy 4). To make it clear that text and multimedia resources are being used, this book employs the term "resource-based inquiry."

## Asking Questions

Reflective educators work with students to create "democratic learning environments" in which "students have the time to explore and find the questions that are most significant in their lives as inquirers" (Short and Burke). This is where inquiry begins—with the big questions. Questions that drive inquiry tend to be complex. If we look at the revised edition of Bloom's taxonomy, most inquiry type questioning would fall into the categories of Apply, Analyze, or Evaluate (numbers 3, 4, and 5 in the Cognitive Processes Dimension of the Taxonomy Table.) Although the Taxonomy Table is not as rigidly hierarchical as Bloom's original, co-author David R. Krathwohl makes clear that the six cognitive process categories do "form a scale from simple to complex" (215).

A higher-level question such as "How could we design a new playground for our school?" cannot be answered by an informational resource. First of all, the question is specific to a particular group of children with a particular teacher, in a particular culture, in a particular climate, with particular monetary constraints and opinions about what a good playground is. Thus, no one can answer the question other than that particular group. Of course, there are objective facts that can help them eventually to answer this big question, but the children will never find these facts by looking at an information source with just the big question in mind.

Figure 2.1 Reflection Points for
Educators Doing Inquiry

# Reflection Points

☐ Are students merely repackaging information?

☐ Are students trying to find the right answer or an answer that meets their needs?

☐ Am I behaving like an expert or a fellow seeker of meaning?

☐ Am I just monitoring inquiry or am I an active participant?

☐ Is this doable?

☐ Is this meaningful?

☐ Is this important?

☐ Are children interested?

☐ Are my students gathering facts or evidence?

☐ Do I use authors' names when modeling new knowledge creation?

☐ Are my students talking?

☐ Are my students interrupting discussions to ask questions?

☐ Are my students directing answers at me or at each other?

☐ Are students comparing and assessing each other's evidence?

☐ Are my students using metacognitive strategies?

☐ Am I allowing students time to sit and think?

☐ Am I allowing my students enough time to just sit and think?

☐ Am I taking time to just sit and think?

☐ Am I asking students to consider their own reflection points?

## Asking Big Questions

Library media specialists know that higher-level questions make for better resource-based inquiry. McKenzie, who produces the educational technology journal *From Now On,* differentiates between trivial questions and essential questions. Essential questions address matters that are important to the student. They take the child from "mere understanding" to "action to solve a problem," thus moving from category 2 (Understand) to category 3 (Apply) in the revised Bloom's Taxonomy. Essential questions cannot be answered with a yes or no. One essential question will lead to another. Essential questions do not have a definite answer. Finally, and most importantly, these questions are interesting to the student.

David V. Loertscher of San Jose State University is well known for his plea that we ban units that are encyclopedic reports and do little or nothing to engage children in real learning. Doug Johnson, the Director of Media and Technology for Mankato Public Schools and a long-time writer on library issues, defines four levels of questions. As one ascends the ladder of question types, student interest increases and projects become more inquiry-based.

Level 1 questions are factual and can be answered by an encyclopedia. The student has no personal connection with a level 1 question. In fact, at this level the subject of research may not even be articulated as a question. For example, a student might say, "My research is about mountain lions."

Level 2 questions will probably require looking at several sources of information. The student will need to marshal evidence to support her conclusions. For example, a student might try to answer the question: "What strategies have mountain lions developed to help them survive?"

Level 3 questions develop a level two question further by making it relevant to the student. To answer this type of question a student will have to consult library resources and perhaps primary documents or displays at local museums and parks. It would be helpful to complement the resource-based inquiry with some hands-on research, such as interviewing local experts or conducting an opinion poll. An example based on the previous question would be: "What can be done to ensure that mountain lions in my state do not go extinct?"

The fourth level transforms this question into a plan of action. It will be useful to government or organizations that want to effect change. An example might be: "What should our state legislature do to protect the mountain lion?"

It is clear that essential questions and level 4 questions are the best questions to guide inquiry. They ensure interest because they are personally relevant to the students. They require an array of resources, both primary and secondary, and hands-on research. They lead to action and involvement by the students. They establish areas of interest that should remain with the students for the rest of their lives.

Once the guiding questions are established, it is necessary to break them down into what I term "resource-ready" questions. These questions are mainly knowledge-level questions. In the Bloom's original taxonomy, knowledge is the lowest educational objective. This does not mean that inquiry is no longer taking place. As the new taxonomy makes clear, knowledge is relevant to all six cognitive processes. While seeking factual answers and setting them within the framework of the Guiding Questions, children will inevitably achieve objectives within all six cognitive processes, such as recalling, summarizing, explaining, interpreting, classifying, organizing, and checking.

Breaking down the big questions is an important information literacy skill that relates to AASL's first information standard: "Learners use skills, resources, and tools to inquire, think critically, and gain knowledge." The key to this standard is the ability to "develop and refine a range of questions to frame the search for new understanding" (AASL 4).

## Asking Resource-Ready Questions

To be successful with information sources, children need to be able to break down the big questions into questions that can be answered at the level of knowledge and comprehension. Only after they have built sufficient knowledge and comprehension can they begin to tackle the bigger, higher-level questions. Note that this cannot be done by information resources alone. Hands-on experimentation, first-hand knowledge, and expert opinions are all necessary. However, many of the bigger questions, once broken down, can be answered by an information source.

The challenge for the library media specialist is to predict how the big questions will break down in order to start building resource lists. For both the teacher and the library media specialist, another challenge is to guide the children to see how the smaller questions are pieces of the puzzle that will eventually help them to develop an answer that is informed by real knowledge. After that, motivation and engagement with the possible answers will bring the creative thinking and problem-solving abilities of the children to the fore.

## Thinking about Questions

Before asking children to deal with particular questions, whether big, essential questions or focused questions for resource-based inquiry, it is useful to consider what we mean by questions. An educator experienced in inquiry-based learning might describe questions in many ways. Figure 2.2 Thinking about Questions, is an example of what an ongoing discussion about questions might produce in the classroom. Of all the types of questions, only the frivolous and abstract are unsuitable for inquiry. Frivolous questions are too silly or slight to be engaging over time. Abstract questions are inappropriate for very young and elementary-aged children, and they do not lend themselves to hands-on investigation. All the other statements in this list are true of inquiry-based questions.

The challenge for schools with a rigidly defined core curriculum is to interpret the core content in such as way that it connects to the real life interests and questions of students. The challenge for more open curricula is to find motivating questions with enough content to sustain interest and propel investigations over time. As long as questions are neither frivolous nor abstract, teachers and children should be able to frame content into questions that are worthy of in-depth investigation and thought.

## Questions in the Context of Resource-Based Inquiry

Once a teacher has received a good question for inquiry, several scenarios may unfold. How the children deal with these questions will determine their need for resources and support from the library program. Collaboration between teacher and library media specialist is thus essential right from the start.

## Figure 2.2 Thinking about Questions

# Questions...

- ☐ can be big or small
- ☐ can be factual
- ☐ can be controversial
- ☐ can be personal
- ☐ can stimulate a desire to know
- ☐ can stimulate a desire to act
- ☐ can help us make our lives meaningful
- ☐ can have many answers
- ☐ can have different but correct answers
- ☐ can be interpreted differently depending on the context of the questioner
- ☐ can have different answers for different people depending on their context
- ☐ encourage discussion
- ☐ require discussion
- ☐ require time to ponder
- ☐ are not answered in books, they are answered in hearts and minds
- ☐ stay with us, we find ourselves thinking about them outside of school

# Questions should not be:

- ☐ frivolous
- ☐ abstract

Educators get nervous when the path ahead does not seem clear. We like to have a sense of where we are leading children in their learning. Though we use models for the inquiry process, the work is never linear. As children begin to think about the big question, one of three scenarios can play out.

Let's consider a popular theme from the area of language arts: heroes or visionary people. A big question related to this theme might be: Who is my personal hero and what influence does he or she have on my life? Curricular needs might narrow the theme to figures from a particular historical period or event, scientists, Black Americans, women, writers, current events, or even other children.

Scenario 1

## Coming Up Empty

In the first scenario, gaps in knowledge are revealed that inhibit discussion and questioning around the theme. Perhaps children can name several heroes but know little beyond the name itself. Children may show no interest in heroes as a theme for inquiry. The idea of heroes may not have any personal connection to them. They may have covered the subject in the past in a way that has made the theme seem boring. They may come up with responses that are frivolous, just to have something to say. These children are ready for inquiry-based learning but with different resources and approaches than the other two groups. These children need inspiration.

Scenario 2

## Discovering Differences

As children discuss the theme of a new inquiry unit, differences of opinion and understanding may appear. If children admire a wide variety of heroes for very different reasons, their understanding of "hero" as a term will result in conflicting ideas and debate. For instance, some children may insist that heroes are limited to people who fight in wars. Others who admire sports heroes will have trouble finding common ground for discussion. Children may find this experience of cognitive dissonance a bit disturbing at first, but it should spur them on to further questions in their effort to resolve the conflict of ideas. These children will need resources to help them clarify their current understandings.

Scenario 3

## Finding Immediate Focus

Children may find immediate focus for many reasons. They may have studied in previous years heroes who they would like to look at again. They may come from a region with a colorful local hero they all know and love. They may already have read interesting biographies from the library or have a strong personal interest in a particular type of hero. Whatever the reason, when children exhibit an interested and informed preference from the start, they have found immediate focus and are ready to elaborate on what they know using resource-based inquiry.

# Tasks in the Context of Resource-Based Inquiry

Resource-based inquiry is made easier by defining the task that is required to keep inquiry happening. Figure 2.3 A Resource-Based Inquiry Model will help children and teachers decide where they are in relation to using resources for inquiry. Elaborative tasks with focus for students and teachers include the following: knowledge checking (ensuring that the agreed upon notions of key ideas and vocabulary are correct); resource checking (ensuring that there are enough potential resources to pursue the investigation); reading or being read to (building knowledge); thinking (assimilating new ideas); talking and listening (sharing and clarifying new knowledge); questioning (determining how new ideas fit with previous ideas); writing (noting important terms and ideas); and planning (developing a schema for the outcome of the investigation). Thus, in the elaborative mode of resource-based inquiry, students are following the established model of inquiry and taking on roles of knowledge checker, reader (or dialogic partner in reading), thinker, talker, listener, writer, and planner. Depending on the final outcome, they ultimately will become a producer—constructing a model, producing a film, leading a discussion. The possibilities are endless and will depend very much on the nature of the questions being pursued.

Clarification tasks for students and teachers include knowledge checking (establishing which ideas have validity and which are misconceptions), feasibility checking (establishing which ideas can be pursued with resources), and terminology checking (determining the key terms and vocabulary needed to uncover more information on this topic). They have taken on the role of checker or manager of a potential project, asking themselves "Is there evidence?," "Can we pursue this?," and "What is the definition?" They then are ready to work on finding focus.

Inspirational tasks for students and teachers include background reading (to build knowledge and interest) and supplementary research activities in the classroom. If interest develops, they may discover differences or find immediate focus.

Reading, especially for younger children, involves listening and discussion, watching, interpreting visual clues, and asking questions. It is a highly interactive and engaging activity that requires lots of scaffolding or support from teachers and librarians. For a detailed discussion on using dialogic reading with young children, see my previous book *Project-Based Inquiry Units for Young Children*.

# Other Supports Needed for Resource-Based Inquiry

The primary role of the library media specialist in resource-based inquiry is in modeling the tasks and roles that are still very new to young children. Providing schema to help with early note-taking and working through simple organizational graphics to represent cycles, comparison, contrast, cause and effect, chronology, sequences, or merely lists or key words, can build early metacognitive models for children. Throughout the inquiry process, both teacher and librarian provide scaffolding to help children decide what to do with questions and evidence, how to note evidence in a way that is usable, and how to put the evidence together into a personal understanding. Older students who are comfortable with note-taking can be given a students organizer such as Figure 2.4 at the end of this chapter.

## Figure 2.3  A Resource-Based Inquiry Model

**A Resource-Based Inquiry Model**

Idea for Inquiry—
Big Question or Theme

*Initial discussion, mapping ideas, questioning*
Children are prompted to recall prior knowledge and experiences related to the theme.
All ideas, terms, guesses, predictions, doubts, and feelings are noted. Very open-ended.

| **Come Up Empty** | **Discover Differences** | **Find Focus** |
|---|---|---|
| Have little prior knowledge<br>Have little interest<br>Have little relevant vocabulary<br>Have no hypothesis<br>Have no plan | Have conflicting ideas<br>Have confusion<br>Have debate<br>Have hypotheses<br>Have contradictions to resolve | Have prior knowledge<br>Have motivation<br>Have questions<br>Have hypotheses<br>Have potential plan of action |

| **STIMULATION** | **CLARIFICATION** | **ELABORATION** |
|---|---|---|
| Stimulate interest through resources such as stories, interactive Web sites, narrative nonfiction, illustrations, art, poetry, video, and other multimedia. Encourage free exploration. | Seek out information resources that provide evidence to support ideas. Establish definitions and vocabulary needed for further investigation. Establish key words and key ideas. | Confirm key words and vocabulary. Pursue informational resources that will provide the best evidence for the plan of action. |

| **Find Focus or Discover Differences** | **Pursue another theme** | **Find Focus** | **Continue with Chosen Inquiry Model** |
|---|---|---|---|

# Inquiry Units and Beyond

The inquiry units in the chapters that follow are organized by core curriculum content areas. Learning and information literacy standards are addressed in each unit. Engaging questions for thematic inquiry are presented with a breakdown of resource-ready questions. Resource lists provide fiction and nonfiction texts to fulfill the needs of teachers and students: to stimulate interest, to raise awareness, and to build the kind of knowledge and understanding necessary for engaged action. Higher level inquiry questions almost always involve taking action. Thus, most begin with "How do I…" "How could I…" or "How should I…" The final stage of the inquiry process thus leads to action: a project, presentation, and beyond school, new ways of living and thinking.

Teachers cannot expect to answer all of the questions that arise in a unit of inquiry. This is normal and, in fact, is indicative of a good unit of inquiry. After sufficient first-hand experiences, discussion, and research, children should be generating questions that are open-ended rather than factual. Open-ended questions can rarely be answered directly and simply, even by an expert. That is why inquiry-based learning involves a process that requires time for answers to unfold.

Even when a unit concludes, there still will be questions that remain, to be explored again and again. This is especially important as children develop intellectually. New questions and perspectives will open up to them as their experience and knowledge of the world grows, and consequently, so will a desire to revisit the themes of past units. Thus, units of inquiry cannot be considered "covered" once and for all—not in preschool and not in grade 5. This is because subjects that are well-suited to inquiry are questions that should occupy us all throughout our lives. They are the big questions, the important questions.

Ultimately inquiry is about lifelong learning. It is about ideas that give our lives meaning and focus, that lead us to areas of professional interest or personal pursuit. They are anything but forgettable. Children who participate in inquiry-based learning taste, for perhaps the first time, questions that will occupy and engage their minds for the rest of their lives.

## Figure 2.4  Student Organizer

### Search Terms and Questions

My overall theme is: _____

_____

My big question or questions are: _____

_____

| Subject words for searching databases |
|---|
| |
| Key phrases for searching the Internet |
| |

| Ask an Expert Questions | Hands-on Questions | Resource-Ready Questions |
|---|---|---|
| | | |

# Chapter 3

# Inquiry into Personal Well-Being

## Integrating Core Curriculum Content into Inquiry-Based Learning

We are all concerned about personal health and safety. Anything we can learn about improving our health and avoiding illness should be of lifelong interest to us all. Teachers in the early and elementary school years are well aware of their dual role to educate and care for children. This makes inquiry into personal well-being a good choice for any school. The inquiry approach promotes not just knowledge but action. By integrating these curriculum standards into an inquiry approach to learning, educators will increase the likelihood of effecting positive changes in behavior and attitudes of students toward personal health. Educators themselves will find that they too will question some of their own behaviors and school policies as they lead the inquiry process into these important issues.

Each unit addresses physical education and health core curriculum standards that are directly relevant to each inquiry. The physical education content standards are ultimately sourced from the publication *Moving into the Future: National Standards for Physical Education* (2nd Edition, 2004) of the American Alliance for Health, Physical Education, Recreation and Dance, a group comprising five national associations, six district associations, and a research consortium. The National Health Education Standards are a subset of the physical education and health standards provided on the Education World® online listing of national standards. Both physical education and health content standards strongly support educating children about maintaining their personal well-being. All standards met by these units of inquiry are listed in a chart at the end of the chapter.

**Play Safe!**
(PreK to K)

## A Good Choice for Inquiry

*Play Safe!* is a relevant and motivating unit of inquiry because young children use school recreational facilities every day. They have preferences for certain kinds of play. They have opinions on how best to play. They sometimes observe behaviors in the playground that are not safe, and they may have personal experience of conflict with others during play. It is a subject of great personal interest to any kindergartener.

Children are given guidelines for safe play, but do they have a chance to discuss the whys and wherefores? Can they articulate why they are asked to behave in certain ways? Do they have skills for avoiding or resolving conflict? Can they distinguish between safe and unsafe behaviors? Do they know the possible consequences of risky behavior? Offering them the opportunity to learn more about play through inquiry will have positive outcomes in terms of curriculum and even longer lasting outcomes for safe and responsible behavior. That makes this inquiry unit an excellent way to kick off a year in pre-kindergarten and kindergarten.

Ask yourself and your colleagues how much you currently know about playground safety. Have faculty read up-to-date handbooks? The more people consider all the potential risks, the more they will want to become informed with the help of their students.

## Background Reading

Playground safety might seem at first to be a simple matter. However, some preparatory background reading will soon reveal that playground safety is an area of real concern for schools. A review of current research and safety advice about playgrounds and safe play will convince teachers that this is a meaty subject for in-depth study by the children, teachers, parents, and administration of the school.

*Safe Kids USA* <http://www.usa.safekids.org> reports that playgrounds are where most childhood injuries happen. While playground accidents are rarely fatal, they can result in serious permanent disability, especially falls from playground equipment. A review of this article and safety tips sheets from this site will establish the important safety issues that children will become aware of during the course of the inquiry. It will also raise awareness about playground inspection needs and assessment of appropriate equipment, surfaces, and regulations covering the playground and other recreational areas at school. The site gives links to many related safety issues

*Handbook for Public Playground Safety* <www.cpsc.gov/CPSCPUB/PUBS/325.pdf> is an excellent guide that includes specific equipment lists and height recommendations for preschoolers. It is in the public domain and is ready for use, though the authoring commission asks to be informed as to how you are using it. Schools with programs for children age 2 through 5 need to ensure that they have separate play areas that are clearly demarcated. A review of current playground facilities is imperative before the school year opens and this unit of inquiry begins. Teachers may discover that there are guidelines that the school needs to adopt. For example, the handbook warns that hood or neck drawstrings on jackets and sweatshirts have resulted in strangulation. School documents should advise parents to remove all drawstrings from children's clothing as a safety precaution. Thus, it makes sense to get the whole school community involved in this unit of inquiry. In preparation for this inquiry, the administration and parents' committee can do a thorough playground review and improvement. They will then become experts who can talk to the students about some of the ways they have made the playground safe. Many of these items could appear throughout the school year. Raising awareness in this way will help the entire school community remain vigilant for new problem areas.

**Hands On**

Ask the students to become "playground inspectors" to test the work of the principal and his parents' safety committee. Children can develop iconic checklists for several of the playground hazards such as sharp points, missing caps, trip hazards, litter, fallen branches, and other dangers present in the playground.

*Tricycle Helmets?* <http://www.helmets.org/trike.htm> is another informative site for background reading. This site from the Bicycle Helmet Safety Institute quotes an article on a national study that suggests that young children who cycle, even on a tricycle, need to wear a helmet. According to the study, there are 200,000 to 300,000 cycles sold for preschoolers every year in the United States. It provides information on appropriate headgear for this age group. An important safety message about not allowing children to wear helmets while playing on playground equipment should be considered as part of the school's safety guidelines.

     *Creating a Safe & Friendly School: Lunchroom, Hallways, Playground, and More…* (Northeast Foundation for Children, 2006) is a professional resource that covers how to use equipment, how to follow rules, how to take turns, and how to avoid injury. It includes a teacher's guide for activities and vocabulary.

*S. A. F. E. Play Areas: Creation, Maintenance, and Renovation* by Donna Thompson, Susan D. Hudson, and Heather M. Olsen (Human Kinetics Publishers, 2007) is written by acknowledged experts and includes a CD-ROM for training teachers and other school staff.

# Unit Overview

An inquiry into safe play at school covers many physical education and health outcomes related to acting responsibly, respecting others, enjoying challenge, plus understanding and acting on health issues. Used as a framework for the inquiry, it suggests courses of action for the assessment stage of the inquiry process. Thus, at the end of the inquiry, children will:

- *present and explain safe playground procedures to students or parents*
- *role-play scenes showing respect for others*
- *role-play scenes showing how to avoid conflict*
- *draw their favorite playground activity and explain why they enjoy it*
- *draw a picture of themselves playing safely*
- *explain how risky behavior can result in injury*
- *construct, with the help of the teacher, a list of good buddy guidelines for the playground*
- *use new knowledge during recreational periods*

# Guiding Questions

How do we avoid injury during play? How do we play safely on equipment? How do we play safely with each other? How do we recognize dangerous behavior? How do we resolve conflict?

# Specific Questions

- How do we swing safely?
- How do we climb ladders safely?
- How do we throw balls safely?
- How do we slide safely?
- How do we stand in line safely?
- Where is it safe to run in the playground?
- What shoes are best for the playground?
- What clothes are best for the playground?
- When do I need a hat in the playground?
- How do we share?
- How do we take turns?
- What do we do when a conflict happens?
- How do we treat others with respect?
- Where must we walk?
- What do we do if we get hurt?
- What do we do if we see someone else is hurt?
- How do we eat outdoors?
- What do we do with our trash outdoors?

- How high should I go?
- How can I hurt myself on the playground?
- What should I watch out for on the playground?
- How will the nurse help me if I get hurt?

## Controlled Vocabulary

- Bullies
- Bullying
- Playgrounds
- Playgrounds safety measures
- Safety
- Schools safety measures
- For particular kinds of activities use outdoor games, tag games.

## Internet-Friendly Phrases

"playground safety"
"playground safety for kids"
"playground safety checklist"
"national playground safety institute"

## Kid-Friendly Categories

Google Directory > Kids and Teens
*Search within*    Health > Emotional Health and Wellbeing > Bullying
             Health > Safety

## Resources for *Play Safe!*

### *Raise Interest and Stimulate Discussion*

*Anthony and the Girls* by Ole Konnecke (Farrar, Straus & Giroux, 2006) offers a droll look at playground interaction between boys and girls. Children will enjoy predicting what will happen after the girls console the tearful Anthony and as a bigger, more confident boy comes along. This is a great discussion starter about how to make friends, how to ask to play together, and how to share, without being preachy. Anthony's antics to get the girls' attention would also serve a discussion about inappropriate use of playground equipment.

*Beegu* by Alexis Deacon (Farrar, Straus & Giroux, 2003) is primarily a story about parental loss and reunion, but the scene where the floppy-eared yellow alien meets children in a playground will stimulate discussion of cooperative, friendly behavior.

*Dancing Dinos Go to School* by Sally Lucas (Random House, 2006) is an easy reader that will delight preschoolers with the riotous behavior of dinosaurs on the school playground.

*Hop! Plop!* by Corey Rosen Schwartz (Walker, 2006) shows two best friends whose mismatched size makes enjoyment of playground equipment nearly impossible. The basic physics of using the playground and humorous story will get children talking about potential mishaps on the playground.

*King of the Playground* by Phyllis Reynold Naylor, illustrated by Nola Langner Malone (Aladdin, 1994), portrays a boy who overcomes his fear of a playground bully.

*Kyle's Recess* [e-book] by Terri Dougherty (Picture Window Books, 2007) has the principal getting all the balls off the roof of the school.

*Martin and the Giant Lions* by Caron Lee Cohen, illustrated by Elizabeth Sayles (Clarion Books, 2002), allows a child to dream about going on the slide that his mother says is just too high. A good choice about what can be done in reality on the playground and what we can do in our imaginations.

*Please Play Safe!: Penguin's Guide to Playground Safety* by Margery Cuyler (Scholastic Press, 2006) makes a good introductory read aloud because the animals in the story do all the wrong things. The narrator asks the question "Is that right?" for each. Children will have fun telling the animals that they are playing dangerously.

*The Recess Queen* by Alexis O'Neill (Scholastic Press, 2002) presents the problem of a playground bully in a non-didactic and exuberant story.

*The Recess Queen* [DVD] (Spoken Arts, 2003) offers the same story narrated with music.

## Resource-Ready Core Collection

*Living Safe, Playing Safe* by Karen W. Olson (Theytus Books, 2005) is a short, easy text with illustrations teaching rules for the playground.

*Look at the Playground!* by Mary Elizabeth Salzmann (ABDO, 2006) is a good choice for emergent readers who need a book with playground-related words.

*Manners on the Playground* by Terri DeGezelle (Capstone Press, 2005) introduces children to all of the important behaviors for getting along with others on the playground. The clear photographs will help discussions of what good behaviors look like.

*My Map Book* by Sara Fanelli (HarperCollins, 1995) has a child-like representation of her playground. This is a good guide for an early exploration of the playground.

*Piggyback Songs* [CD] (Kimbo Educational, 1995) includes "We've Been Playing on the Playground" and other school songs.

*The Playground* [e-book] by Jacquelin Laks Gorman (Weekly Reader Early Learning Library, 2005) has clear images of children using playground areas and equipment appropriate to kindergarten children.

*The Playground Problem* by Margaret McNamara (Aladdin, 2004) is an easy reader with an absorbing playground conflict.

*Playground Push-Around* [videorecording] (Boulden, 1999) is a 5-minute video that offers a scenario for children to discuss. The 8-minute version includes a counselor's comments.

*Playground Safety* [DVD] (100% Educational Videos, 2004) is a 15-minute video that talks about how to prevent accidents on the playground–good preparation for role plays. It also teaches how to use playground equipment properly, follow playground rules, take turns, and reduce injuries.

*Playground Safety* by Peggy Pancella (Heinemann Library, 2005) is written in simple, accessible text for kindergarten readers.

*Playgrounds* by Wendy Sadler (Heinemann Library, 2005) discusses what playground equipment is made of and why.

*Safety First* by Rebecca Weber (Compass Point Books, 2004) describes safety in the home, school, and playground.

*Safety on the Playground and Outdoors* [e-book] by Lucia Raatma (Child's World, 2005) is written for older children, but the pictures will inspire discussion and the tips can stimulate ideas about the children's own playground, such as the type of surfaces they recommend.

*Safety on the Playground* by Lucia Raatma (Bridgestone Books, 1999) looks at safety using swings, slides, and other playground equipment. Children will find this accessible with a reader.

**Hands On**

After children have explored the playground with inquiry in mind, have them create a map based on the playground map example in My Map Book.

## Resource-Ready Supplementary Collection

*Around the World Games* by Margaret Hall (Heinemann Library, 2002)

*A Kid's Guide to Staying Safe at Playgrounds* by Maribeth Boelts (PowerKids Press, 1997)

*Kids Talk about Bullying* [e-book] by Carrie Finn (Picture Window Books, 2007)

*Let's Jump Rope* by Sarah Hughes (Children's Press, 2000)

*Let's Play Hopscotch* by Sarah Hughes (Children's Press, 2000)

*Let's Play Tag* by Sarah Hughes (Children's Press, 2000)

*Living Safe, Playing Safe* by Karen W. Olson, illustrated by Leonard George, Jr. (Theytus Books, 2005)

*Playground Survival* by Peggy Burns, illustrated by Deborah Allwright (Raintree, 2005)

*School Safety* [e-book] by Lucia Raatma (Child's World, 2004)

**Allergy Alert!**
*(Grades 1 to 2)*

## A Good Choice for Inquiry

*Allergy Alert!* is a relevant and motivating unit of inquiry because children suffer from food allergies and sensitivities, allergies to pollen or other airborne particles, and allergies to insects, plants, or other environmental factors. Children naturally ask questions when they see a friend use a puffer, wear a medical alert bracelet, or carry an EpiPen®. They wonder why a child cannot run in physical education class. They are upset that their school has banned peanut butter sandwiches. They hear medical terms used that they do not understand. All of these observations make children curious about allergies as they relate to others.

Children with allergies want to be understood and have their needs recognized. Thus, even those children who do not have allergies must be aware of the potentially harmful effects of allergens on their friends and peers. Raising awareness through guiding inquiry will ensure that children develop empathy for other children who must deal with allergies and use safe practices themselves.

## Background Reading

Though we commonly speak of food allergies, asthma, and hives with children, do we truly understand how allergens work? It makes fascinating reading for adults who have not had occasion to explore the science of allergies. Thanks to child-friendly resources, it can also be a theme of inquiry with children in grades 1 and 2.

It is estimated that 15 to 20 percent of American adults have some kind of allergy, and most begin in childhood. In fact, allergies "rank first among children's chronic diseases" (American College of Allergy, Asthma, and Immunology).

Background reading can reveal frightening stories of sudden death from anaphylaxis after eating seemingly harmless foods or from insect bites. It is an issue that educators cannot ignore. Incorporating this theme into a unit of inquiry can help to educate teachers and children, and get parents involved as well. As with all good inquiry units, the educators will be sure to learn something. You think a peanut is a nut? Read on!

*Auckland Allergy Clinic* <http://www.allergyclinic.co.nz/guides/1.html> "What is an Allergy?" that explains the science behind what happens during an allergic reaction. Links to specific allergies are provided.

*Caring for Your Child with Severe Food Allergies: Emotional Support and Practical Advice* from a Parent Who's Been There by Lisa Cipriano Collins (John Wiley & Sons, 2000) is another good resource for parents. It discusses how parents can work with schools and teachers to raise awareness and increase safety for allergic children.

*Dealing with Food Allergies in Babies and Children* by Janice Vickerstaff Joneja (Bull Publishing, 2007) is a good library resource for parents of allergic children with many tips and strategies for educators as well. The book focuses on the top 10 allergens among children.

*Fit Kids: A Practical Guide to Raising Active and Healthy Children—From Birth to Teens* by Mary L. Gavin (DK Publishing, 2004) has a section on nutrition and food allergies.

*The Food Allergy & Anaphylaxis Network* <http://www.foodallergy.org> gives the latest information on food allergy issues. Free programs for schools are available through the site.

*How Stuff Works "Diseases Channel"* <http://health.howstuffworks.com/diseases-channel.htm> has an 11-part article covering "Allergy Basics."

*Kids Health* <http://kidshealth.org/kid/health_problems/allergiesimmune/food_allergies.html> is a good explanation of what happens to the mast cell during an allergic reaction.

*Medem Medical Library* <http://www.medem.com/medlb/medlib_entry.cfm> includes a link to "Asthma and Other Allergies" listing all of the potential allergies and related problems that educators might encounter with children.

*The Whole Foods Allergy Cookbook: Two Hundred Gourmet & Homestyle Recipes for the Food Allergic Family* by Cybele Pascal (Vital Health Publishing, 2006) is a great teacher's resource for safe food preparation in the classroom and for this unit of inquiry in particular.

## Unit Overview

An inquiry into allergies covers many health outcomes related to personal health behaviors, knowledge of personal health needs, influences on health, and the importance of personal health goals. By the end of the inquiry, children will:

- create puppet presentations about allergies for other children (describing what the puppet is allergic to, how it affects them, and how the puppet deals with it)
- role play prepared scenarios involving allergies for other students in class (and ask other children to discuss appropriate responses)
- inform students throughout the school about how to deal with allergies through posters and signs
- challenge other children to take the FaanKids "Avoid the Allergen" test for one day

**Ask an Expert**

Have children invite a health professional of their choice to view the puppet shows and posters.

# Guiding Questions

What kinds of allergies can children have? What can we do to help children with allergies? Why do we get allergies? How do allergies work?

# Specific Questions

- What are the symptoms of allergies?
- What foods are children sometimes allergic to?
- Are allergies dangerous?
- What medicines do children take for allergies?
- Can you grow out of your allergy?
- Are allergies for life?
- Can allergies get better?
- Can allergies be cured?
- Why do we get allergies?
- What is an EpiPen®?
- What is a Medical Alert bracelet?

# Controlled Vocabulary

- Allergy
- Food allergy
- Insect allergy

# Internet-Friendly Phrases

- "food allergies"
- "insect allergies"
- "common allergies" children

# Kid-Friendly Categories

Google Directory >    Kids and Teens
*Search within Health* >  Conditions and Diseases > Allergies

# Resources for *Allergy Alert!*

## *Raise Interest and Stimulate Discussion*

*Aaron's Awful Allergies* by Troon Harrison (Kids Can Press, 1996) retells the emotional
  story of a boy who must give up his beloved pets due to allergies.
*Alexander the Elephant Who Couldn't Eat Peanuts* [videorecording] (Food Allergy Network, n.d.)

*Aneil Has a Food Allergy* by Jillian Powell (Chelsea Clubhouse, 2005) is a good book to personalize the concept of food allergy. The librarian or teacher might wish to narrate his or her own version of Aneil's story to make it more accessible. This book is an ideal candidate for a nonfiction dialogic reading.

*Emma's Strange Pet* by Jean Little (HarperCollins, 2003) is an easy reader about a girl with allergies who tries a lizard as an alternative to the usual furry pets. This is a good book for a classroom collection during this inquiry.

*FaanKids* <http://www.fankids.org> contains many activities for children that fit the core curriculum outcomes for this inquiry. Go to the "Clubhouse" to get good discussion-starter statements from children about their allergies and how they deal with them.

*The Peanut Butter Jam* by Elizabeth Sussman Nassau, illustrated by Margot Janet Ott (Health Press, 2001), tells the story of a boy with a peanut allergy who puts himself in danger.

*The Peanut-Free Café* by Gloria Koster (A. Whitman, 2006) is a great story for discussion since it is the kids in the story who come up with a creative solution to help a new boy with a peanut allergy feel welcome.

*Up the President's Nose* by Scott Nickel (Stone Arch Books, 2008) will appeal to boys who like a Captain Underpants approach to information. A tiny Jimmy Sniffles goes up a leader's nose to fight allergens.

**Sharing**

Use the animal characters in the FaanKids "International Zoo" to inspire students to present information about allergies through their puppet show summative assessment.

## Resource-Ready Core Collection

*Allergies* by Sharon Gordon (Children's Press, 2003) is a simple, accessible text about common allergens and their side effects.

*Allergies* by Jillian Powell (Cherrytree Books, 2007) includes frequently asked questions about allergies.

*Allergies* by Angela Royston (Heinemann Library, 2004) has good photos and diagrams and covers most questions about allergies. Most children will need mediation with some of the text.

*Allergies: I Think I Am Going to Sneeze* by Pat Thomas and Lesley Harker (Barrons, 2008) is written for young children to help them understand that allergies can be controlled.

*Eating* by Claire Llewellyn (Smart Apple Media, 2005) is a simple text with a section on food allergies.

*FaanKids* <http://www.fankids.org> reviews "Food Allergy Basics" with symptoms, treatments, and tips.

*Food Allergies* by Jason Glaser (Capstone Press, 2007) is a guide to food allergies with appealing photos of children and easy-to-read text. It includes recipes.

*Let's Talk about Having Allergies* by Elizabeth Weitzman (PowerKids Press, 1997) is an accessible text with good information on how children must be prepared to deal with their allergies at all times.

*Staying Well* by John Burstein (Gareth Stevens, 2007) covers many health topics in a child-friendly way, including allergy and asthma attacks.

*What Should We Eat?* by Angela Royston (Heinemann Library, 2006) is a simple guide to food that includes information on food allergies.

## UNIT 3: *An Ounce of Prevention*
*(Grades 3 to 4)*

## A Good Choice for Inquiry

It happens every year, in every school around the world: children come to school with a cold or flu, and then everyone gets sick. Children often don't understand why they need to stay home when they are sick. Repeated reminders to cover their mouths, use tissues, to keep items out of their mouths can fall on deaf ears because children don't understand why these demands are being made.

It is easy to transform the word "germ" from a nag word to a visually compelling idea by using the many child-friendly resources that exist about infections and the common cold. Children are naturally drawn to subjects related to their bodily functions, despite—and sometimes because of—the "yuck" factor. Once their interest is sparked, they will be keen to devise good hygiene strategies to avoid the microorganisms that make us sick.

## Background Reading

Colds and flu arrive every year in the classroom. Teachers have their own strategies for helping prevent infection, but how effective are they? Do teachers and librarians fully understand the process of infection? Can they describe how a germ works? Do they really know what germs are?

A topic as common as the common cold can lead educators to their own discovery process. Few of us have escaped growing up with some old wives' tale of how to prevent or help a cold or other infection. But how accurate is our knowledge? Some background will tell us.

*The Everything Parent's Guide to Childhood Illnesses: Expert Advice that Dispels Myths and Helps Parents Recognize Symptoms and Understand Treatments* (Adams Media, 2007)

*The Good Doctor's Guide to Colds and Flu* [e-book] by Neil Schachter (PerfectBound, 2005) looks at common infections and includes information related to children.
*Infections* <www.kidshealth.org/parent/infections/> from the parents' section of Kids Health offers a good overview of all the common infections of childhood.

## Unit Overview

An inquiry into preventing sickness covers health outcomes related to health promotion, disease prevention, health products, health services, plus the importance of setting personal goals and communicating about health issues. At the end of the inquiry, children will:

■ develop and deliver a school-wide campaign to educate children about good hygiene

# Guiding Questions

What can we do to prevent ourselves from catching colds and other infections? Why do we get sick?

# Specific Questions

- What do germs do inside our body?
- What do germs look like?
- Where do germs come from?
- Can germs kill us?
- Will regular soap get rid of germs?
- What parts of our bodies can be attacked by germs?
- Who discovered germs?
- How do we get rid of germs once they are in our body?
- Where do germs live (when they aren't in us)?

# Controlled Vocabulary

- Bacteria
- Cleanliness
- Communicable diseases
- Hygiene
- Immune System
- Immunity
- Immunization
- Microorganisms
- Viruses
- For particular kinds of illnesses use Cold (Disease), Mumps.

# Internet-Friendly Phrases

- "infectious diseases"
- "contagious diseases"
- "preventing flu"
- "stay healthy"
- "good hygiene"

# Kid-Friendly Categories

Google Directory >       Kids and Teens
*Search within*          Health

# Resources for *An Ounce of Prevention*

## *Raise Interest and Stimulate Discussion*

*Andrew Lost in Uncle Al* by J.C. Greenburg (Random House, 2007) is a possible novel read aloud to accompany the unit of inquiry.

*Blecch! Icky, Sticky, Gross Stuff in Your School* [e-book] by Pam Rosenberg, illustrated by Beatriz Helena Ramos (Child's World, 2008), is a great book for projecting on a wall to read together. With information on bacteria, fungus, germs, mold, and viruses, it is a yucky romp through all kinds of surprising science tidbits related to germ theory. Questions like "What has more bacteria—a toilet seat or a school cafeteria tray?" will make children want to know more about staying germ-free.

*Germs* by Ross Collins (Bloomsbury Children's Books, 2004) offers a silly story with characters with gross-out names like Snot, Pus, Rash, and Scab. A good choice to attract reluctant readers, it will get children laughing and talking about this serious scientific theme.

*The Giant Germ* by Anne Capeci, illustrated by John Speirs (Scholastic, 2000), has Ms. Frizzle's class encountering a larger-than-life microbe.

## *Resource-Ready Core Collection*

*All about Health and Hygiene* [DVD] (Schlessinger Media, 2006) is a 23-minute informational video about hygiene and bacteria and offers an experiment for children to try.

*Bill Nye the Science Guy's Great Big Book of Tiny Germs* by Bill Nye (Hyperion Books for Children, 2005) offers answers to any question children might have about germs, especially about how germs are transmitted from one kid to another. These books have high kid appeal and solid scientific information, making them a good choice at this age for an answer resource.

*The Common Cold* by Terry Allan Hicks (Marshall Cavendish, 2006) covers all aspects of the common cold—biology, history, and treatment—and includes a case study of someone suffering from a cold.

*Dirty and Clean* by Melinda Lilly (Rourke Publishing, 2004) presents introductory concepts and simple science experiments to build knowledge for this inquiry.

*Germ Zappers* by Fran Balkwill, illustrated by Mic Rolph (Cold Spring Harbor Laboratory Press, 2002), explains what bacteria, viruses, and other germs do in the body and how our body fights back with the help of special cells.

*Germs* [DVD] (Disney Educational Productions, 2003) is a Bill Nye creation about the germ theory of disease, including his usual experimental demonstrations.

*Germs* by Judy Oetting, illustrated by Tad Herr (Children's Press, 2006), is a simple text for children with reading difficulties.

*Germs Make Me Sick!* by Melvin Berger, illustrated by Marylin Hafner (HarperCollins, 1995), is a classic in children's nonfiction that describes how infections are spread and how our bodies fight back.

*Healing and Medicine* by Gerry Bailey (Picture Window Books, 2005) looks at ways to prevent infection.

*Hygiene and Health* by Claire Llewellyn (QED Publishing, 2006) is an easy-to-read nonfiction book with activities for classroom use.

*Infection, Detection, Protection* <http://www.amnh.org/nationalcenter/infection/index.html> from the American Museum of Natural History offers interactive games and activities about microorganisms and the fight against infectious disease.

*Keep Clean: A Look at Hygiene* by Katie Bagley (Bridgestone Books, 2002) is a book for struggling readers.

*Keep Healthy!* by Angela Royston (Heinemann Library, 2003) covers the basics about germs.

*Keeping Clean: Handwashing for Health* [DVD] (100% Educational, 2003) explains why handwashing is important and presents experiments.

*Life in the Human Body* by Jill Bailey (Raintree, 2003) introduces microlife in our skin, hair, blood, mouth, and intestines.

*Microlife That Makes Us Ill* by Steve Parker (Raintree, 2006) covers bugs and worms as well as germs, so it may confuse some students, but the double-page spreads make it easy to direct children to the right information.

*Oh Yuck!: The Encyclopedia of Everything Nasty* by Joy Masoff, illustrated by Terry Sirrell (Workman, 2000), is a reference book that can be dipped into throughout the inquiry process.

*Personal Hygiene* by Alexandra Powe Allred (Perfection Learning, 2005) has sections on how germs spread disease, why you should brush your teeth, and the importance of washing hands.

*Personal Hygiene and Good Health* by Shirley W. Gray (Child's World, 2004) relates good hygiene to germ theory.

*Prevention and Good Health* [e-book] by Shirley W. Gray (Child's World, 2004) has a chapter devoted to how germs spread. Its narrative style makes it a good book for classroom exploration.

*Staying Healthy* by Angela Royston (Raintree, 2004) uses a comparison with animal behavior to look at how humans stay healthy and avoid germs.

*Staying Healthy Good Hygiene* by Alice B. McGinty, illustrated by Seth Dinnerman (Franklin Watts, 1998), is an accessible look at avoiding germs.

*Under a Microscope: Small Life* by Helen Lepp Friesen (Perfection Learning, 2006) gives elementary students a look at microscope life.

*What Are Germs* by Alvin Silverstein, Virginia Silverstein, and Laura Silverstein Nunn, illustrated by Rick Stromoski (Franklin Watts, 2002), uses cartoons to assist understanding.

*What's Living in Your Classroom?* by Andrew Solway (Heinemann Library, 2006) features many microorganisms, including those that cause colds and flu.

*Why Is Hand Washing So Important?* <kidshealth.org/parent/firstaid_safe/home/hand_washing.html> relates hand washing to prevention of the common cold and serious infectious diseases.

*Why Should I Brush My Teeth?: And Other Questions about Healthy Teeth* by Louise Spilsbury (Heinemann Library, 2003) includes information on caries.

*Why Should I Wash My Body?: And Other Questions about Keeping Clean and Healthy* by Louise Spilsbury (Heinemann Library, 2003) touches on hygiene issues in detail on double-page spreads featuring a question-and-answer format.

*Why Should I Wash My Hair?: And Other Questions about Healthy Skin and Hair* by Louise Spilsbury (Heinemann Library, 2003) deals with hygiene related to skin and hair.

*World's Worst Germs* by Anna Claybourne (Raintree, 2006) answers a common question during inquiry—which germs are the worst? Nine major illnesses, their prevention and their treatment are presented in an entertaining way.

## Resource-Ready Supplementary Collection

*Achoo!: The Most Interesting Book You'll Ever Read about Germs* by Trudee Romanek, illustrated by Rose Cowles (Kids Can Press, 2003)

*Chicken Pox* by Angela Royston (Heinemann Library, 2002)

*Colds* by Angela Royston, illustrations by Jeff Edwards (Heinemann Library, 2002)

*Fifth Disease* by Elizabeth Laskey (Heinemann Library, 2003)

*Flu* by Elizabeth Laskey (Heinemann Library, 2003)

*Impetigo* by Elizabeth Laskey (Heinemann Library, 2003)

*Mumps* by Elizabeth Laskey (Heinemann Library, 2003)

*Pinkeye* by Angela Royston (Heinemann Library, 2002)

*Whooping Cough* by Elizabeth Laskey (Heinemann Library, 2003)

# I'm on the Right Track to Health
*(Grades 5 to 6)*

## A Good Choice for Inquiry

Physical fitness is a major health issue for children in developing countries around the world. With increased time spent playing video games, surfing the Internet, and watching TV, there are fewer opportunities and more distractions for children than ever before. Our cities promote the use of cars to get from point A to point B, especially in cities with urban sprawl. Although the rise of obesity is obviously a related issue, it is a sensitive issue for some pre-teens as well as a topic for personal change that may require medical intervention and advice. Thus, it is more appropriate to focus on the physical fitness aspects of health with the physical education subject specialists already at the school.

It is vital for children to think about their own physical health and fitness now, when they are at an age to change habits that can become entrenched for life. They are old enough to be able to take on a personal project that will have components outside of regular classes and library research time.

There are many excellent books and videos on physical fitness available for children in this age group. Students who focus on unusual physical fitness activities may need to seek further information in the Internet categories and Web sites listed below. Specific searches in subscription databases will yield good results as well.

## Background Reading

There is probably no staff room in the developed world where teachers have not discussed the growing problem of physically unfit children. However, a little learning is a dangerous thing. Background reading can help to dispel any misconceptions or misinformation that we may have on this issue. It can also provide statistics and medical knowledge for a rousing start to the topic in the classroom.

*Active Start for Healthy Kids: Activities, Exercises, and Nutritional Tips* by Stephen J. Virgilio (Human Kinetics, 2006) is a practice guide to teaching children about physical fitness. It includes sections on rhythm, movement, and yoga.

*Adapted Games & Activities: From Tag to Team Building* by Pattie Rouse (Human Kinetics, 2004) will give teachers ideas about fun games to get children exercising and thinking about what they like to do best.

*Athletic Fitness for Kids* by Scott B. Lancaster (Human Kinetics, 2008) is a new book about building a fitness program for children.

*Fit Kids: A Practical Guide to Raising Active and Healthy Children—From Birth to Teens* by Mary L. Gavin (DK Publishing, 2004) offer strategies to use with children, including children who are already athletes.

*No Gym? No Problem!: Physical Activities for Tight Spaces* by Charmain Sutherland (Human Kinetics, 2006) has more than 100 games that meet standards for physical education yet can be done outside of the gymnasium.

*NYC Program Gets Kids Up and Running* by Karen Matthews <http://www.usatoday.com/news/health/2007-10-21-3653440333_x.htm> is a news story to show teachers what is possible.

## Unit Overview

An inquiry into maintaining a healthy body covers physical education and health outcomes related to physical activity, personal fitness, respect, challenge, and prevention. At the end of the inquiry, children will:

■ Make a personal plan for fitness
■ Monitor their progress
■ Keep a diary of their progress (video, sound, photo diary, written, Web page, presentation software)

## Guiding Questions

How can I make a personal fitness plan that I can stick to? What should my plan include? What information observations should I make to monitor my own progress?

## Specific Questions

■ What sports or types of exercise best fit my personality and habits?
■ What is a realistic fitness goal?
■ How many times should I exercise per week?
■ What are the best forms of exercise for weight loss?
■ What are the best forms of exercise for building endurance?
■ What are the best forms of exercise for building strong muscles?
■ Can I target specific areas of my body during exercise?
■ Do I need to see a doctor before I begin a physical fitness program?
■ What are my current physical fitness strengths?
■ What does a personal physical fitness plan look like?
■ What are some cool sports that I may not know anything about?
■ How will exercise improve my overall health?
■ Can I hurt myself while exercising?
■ How does my diet affect my fitness plan?

## Controlled Vocabulary

- Exercise
- Muscular system
- Physical education and training
- Physical fitness
- Skeleton
- For particular kinds of sports use Badminton, Gymnastics, Swimming.

## Internet-Friendly Phrases

- "physical fitness"
- "working out"

## Kid-Friendly Categories

Google Directory >    Kids and Teens
*Search within*      Health > Fitness

## Resources for *I'm on the Right Track to Health*

### *Raise Interest and Stimulate Discussion*

*Homeroom Exercise* by Jana Striegal (Holiday House, 2002) will appeal to girls who enjoy a sad but hopeful story.

*Run for It* by Robert Hirschfeld (Little, Brown, 2002) tells the story of an overweight 13-year-old boy who is helped by a friend to persevere in running a race for cancer.

*World's Oldest Dragon* by Kate McMullan, illustrated by Bill Basso (Grosset & Dunlap, 2006) deals with the theme of physical fitness.

 **Sharing** — Use these texts in group literature circles to get children talking about physical fitness and exercise.

### *Resource-Ready Core Collection*

*24 Hour Fitness Centers: Fitness Articles* <http://www.24hourfitness.com/FitnessArticles.do> lists a wide variety of articles on how and why to exercise, including common "lies and myths."

*Active Kids* by Kathryn Smithyman and Bobbie Kalman, photographs by Marc Crabtree (Crabtree Publishing Company, 2003), covers the benefits of exercise and fun activities to increase strength, endurance, and flexibility.

*Bend and Stretch: Learning about Your Bones and Muscles* [e-book] by Pamela Hill Nettleton, illustrated by Becky Shipe (Picture Window Books, 2004), is an easy reader aimed at younger children, but the clear explanations and drawings make this a worthwhile resource for struggling readers.

*Body and Mind* by Jeannie Kim (Scholastic, 2003) is a guide to many health topics, including exercise.

*Body Talk: The Straight Facts on Fitness, Nutrition and Feeling Great about Yourself* by Ann Douglas and Julie Douglas, illustrations by Claudia Davila (Maple Tree Press, 2006), looks at fitness and body image for girls in a positive way.

*Build Your Bones* <http://www.childrensmuseum.org/special_exhibits/bones/kids_mazeGame.htm> is an excellent interactive game to help children learn how exercise builds healthy bones.

*Denise Austin's Fit Kids* [DVD] (Lions Gate Home Entertainment, 2004) is a workout combining exercises as diverse as yoga and hip-hop.

*Exercise by the Numbers* by Cecilia Minden (Cherry Lake Publishing, 2008) explains how basic math can help with a fitness program.

*Exercising for Good Health* [e-book] by Shirley W. Gray (Child's World, 2004) explains the whys and wherefores of being fit.

*Fitness* by Bonnie Graves (LifeMatters, 2000) gives good advice about overcoming external and internal barriers to sticking with a fitness program.

*Gross and Cool Body* <http://yucky.discovery.com/flash/> links to a drop-down menu of all body systems.

*Gymnastics Training and Fitness: Being Your Best* by Jen Jones (Capstone Press, 2007) offers expert instructions on keeping fit through gymnastics.

*Jump into a Healthy Life* <http://library.thinkquest.org/5407/> is a think quest linking a healthy heart to jumping rope. Illustrated information on techniques and solid information about the heart and circulatory system is included.

*Keeping Fit* by Barbara Sheen (Heinemann Library, 2008) is an all-purpose guide to fitness.

*KidsHealth for Kids: Nutrition & Fitness Center* <http://www.kidshealth.org/kid/centers/nutrition_center.html>

*My Body* (Shockwave Version) <http://www.kidshealth.org/kid/body/mybody_SW.html> has lots of appeal for this age group and covers all body systems related to exercise.

*Physical Activity (BAM! Body and Mind)* <http://www.bam.gov/sub_physicalactivity/index.html> has high appeal for pre-teens and excellent interactive tools for finding the perfect physical fitness for each student.

*Physical Activity* by Alexandra Powe Allred (Perfection Learning, 2005) discusses the importance of regular exercise.

*Staying Healthy, Let's Exercise* by Alice B. McGinty (PowerKids Press, 1997) relates healthy bones, lungs, and heart to getting exercise. Examples of good exercises are provided.

*Tai Chi for Kids* by Jose Figueroa and Stephan Berwick, illustrations by Stephanie Tok (Tuttle Publishing, 2005), gives step-by-step directions with illustrations.

*Why Should I Eat This Carrot?: And Other Questions about Healthy Eating* by Louise Spilsbury (Heinemann Library, 2003) uses a question-and-answer format to address information on how to make healthy food choices.

*Why Should I Get Off the Couch?: And Other Questions about Health and Exercise* by Louise Spilsbury (Heinemann Library, 2003) uses question and answer format to teach kids about fitness.

*Work Out with Sonny & Pedro!: Walk, Dance & Stretch Your Way to Fitness* [DVD] (Iris Media, 2006) is a workout video for grades 3 through 6.

Students can learn about the importance of BMI by using the calculator on <http://www.kidshealth.org/kid/nutrition/weight/bmi.html>. Alternatively, ask a doctor to come in for a session. This will be the basis of their goal setting.

Get the students to use the BAM! "Activity Calendar" page to help them create their personal exercise plan. This interactive and printable calendar has a long list of physical activities to choose from, many of which have links to "Activity Cards" with further information. Each link specifies the areas of the body to benefit from the exercise. "Links" and "Sources" open listings of further Web pages.

## *Resource-Ready Supplementary Collection*

*Aerobic Instructor* [videorecording] (TMW Media Group, 2005)

*Be Healthy! It's a Girl Thing: Food, Fitness, and Feeling Great* by Lillian Wai-Yin Cheung (Crown, 2003)

*Exercise* by Beverley Goodger (Smart Apple Media, 2006)

*The Facts about Steroids* by Suzanne LeVert (Benchmark, 2005)

*Food for Fuel: The Connection between Food and Physical Activity* by Betsy Dru Tecco (Rosen Publishing, 2005)

*How to Improve at Swimming* by Paul Mason (Crabtree, 2008)

*Move Your Bones* by Lynette Evans (Children's Press, 2008)

*Real Fitness: 101 Games and Activities to Get Girls Going!* by American Girl, illustrated by Carol Yoshizumi (Pleasant Company Publications, 2006)

*Skate!: Your Guide to Inline, Aggressive, Vert, Street, Roller Hockey, Speed Skating, Dance, Fitness Training, and More* by Michael Shafran (National Geographic Society, 2003)

## Figure 3.1  Standards for Unit 1—*Play Safe!*

| Health |
|---|
| NPH-H.K-4.1 Health Promotion and Disease Prevention |
| Explain how childhood injuries can be prevented. |
| NPH-H.K-4.3 Reducing Health Risks |
| Compare behaviors that are safe to those that are risky or harmful. |
| Develop injury prevention and management strategies for personal health. |
| Demonstrate ways to avoid and reduce threatening situations. |
| NPH-H.K-4.5 Using Communication Skills to Promote Health |
| Differentiate between negative and positive behaviors used in conflict situations. |
| Demonstrate non-violent strategies to resolve conflicts. |
| NPH-H.K-4.7 Health Advocacy |
| Express information and opinions about health issues. |
| Demonstrate the ability to influence and support others in making positive health choices. |

| Physical Education |
|---|
| NPH.K-12.5 Responsible Behavior |
| Demonstrate personal and social behavior in physical activity settings. |
| NPH.K-12.6 Respect for Others |
| Demonstrate understanding and respect for differences among people in physical activity settings. |
| NPH.K-12.7 Understanding Challenge |
| Understand that physical activity provides opportunities for enjoyment, challenge, self-expression, and social interaction. |

## Figure 3.2 Standards for Unit 2—*Allergy Alert!*

| Health |
|---|
| NPH-H.K-4.1 Health Promotion and Disease Prevention |
| Describe relationships between personal health behaviors and individual well-being. |
| Identify common health problems of children. |
| NPH-H.K-4.3 Reducing Health Risks |
| Compare behaviors that are safe to those that are risky or harmful. |
| Demonstrate ways to avoid and reduce threatening situations. |
| Identify responsible health behaviors. |
| Identify personal health needs. |
| Demonstrate strategies to improve or maintain personal health. |
| NPH-H.K-4.4 Influences on Health |
| Describe ways technology can influence personal health. |
| Explain how information from school and family influences health. |
| NPH-H.K-4.5 Using Communication Skills to Promote Health |
| Describe characteristics needed to be a responsible friend and family member. |
| Demonstrate ways to communicate care, consideration, and respect of self and others. |
| NPH-H.K-4.6 Setting Goals for Good Health |
| Demonstrate the ability to apply a decision-making process to health issues and problems. |
| NPH-H.K-4.7 Health Advocacy |
| Express information and opinions about health issues. |
| Demonstrate the ability to influence and support others in making positive health choices. |
| Describe a variety of methods to convey accurate health information and ideas. |
| Identify community agencies that advocate for healthy individuals, families, and communities. |

Figure 3.3

## Standards for Unit 3—
### *An Ounce of Prevention*

| Health |
|---|
| NPH-H.K-4.1 Health Promotion and Disease Prevention |
| Describe relationships between personal health behaviors and individual well being. |
| Explain how childhood illnesses can be prevented or treated. |
| Identify common health problems of children. |
| Describe the basic structure and functions of the human body systems. |
| Describe how physical, social, and emotional environments influence personal health. |
| Identify health problems that should be detected and treated early. |
| NPH-H.K-4.2 Health Information, Products, and Services |
| Demonstrate the ability to locate resources from home, school, and community that provide valid health information. |
| Demonstrate the ability to locate school and community health helpers. |
| NPH-H.K-4.3 Reducing Health Risks |
| Compare behaviors that are safe to those that are risky or harmful. |
| Identify responsible health behaviors. |
| Identify personal health needs. |
| Demonstrate strategies to improve or maintain personal health. |
| NPH-H.K-4.4 Influences on Health |
| Describe ways technology can influence personal health. |
| NPH-H.K-4.5 Using Communication Skills to Promote Health |
| Describe characteristics needed to be a responsible friend and family member. |
| NPH-H.K-4.6 Setting Goals for Good Health |
| Predict outcomes of positive health decisions. |
| NPH-H.K-4.7 Health Advocacy |
| Express information and opinions about health issues. |
| Demonstrate the ability to influence and support others in making positive health choices. |
| Describe a variety of methods to convey accurate health information and ideas. |

# Figure 3.4 Standards for Unit 4—
## *I'm on the Right Track to Health*

| Health |
|---|
| NPH-H.5-8.1 Health Promotion and Disease Prevention |
| Explain the relationship between positive health behaviors and the prevention of injury, illness, disease, and premature death. |
| Describe the interrelationship of mental, emotional, social, and physical health during adolescence. |
| Explain how health is influenced by the interaction of body systems. |
| Describe how family and peers influence the health of adolescents. |
| Analyze how environment and personal health are interrelated. |
| Describe ways to reduce risks related to adolescent health problems. |
| Describe how lifestyle, pathogens, family history, and other risk factors are related to the cause or prevention of disease and other health problems. |
| NPH-H.5-8.2 Health Information, Products and Services |
| Analyze the validity of health information, products, and services. |
| Demonstrate the ability to utilize resources from home, school, and community that provide valid health information. |
| NPH-H.5-8.3 Reducing Health Risks |
| Develop an understanding of the structure of the earth system. |
| Analyze a personal health assessment to determine health strengths and risks. |
| Demonstrate strategies to improve or maintain personal and family health. |
| NPH-H.5-8.4 Influences on Health |
| Analyze how messages from media and other sources influence health behaviors. |
| NPH-H.5-8.6 Setting Goals for Good Health |
| Demonstrate the ability to apply a decision-making process to health issues and problems individually and collaboratively. |
| Analyze how health-related decisions are influenced by individuals, family, and community values. |
| Predict how decisions regarding health behaviors have consequences for self and others. |
| Apply strategies and skills needed to attain personal health goals. |
| Describe how personal health goals are influenced by changing information, abilities, priorities, and responsibilities |
| Develop a plan that addresses personal strengths, needs, and health risks. |

| Physical Education |
|---|
| NPH.K-12.3 Physical Activity |
| Exhibit a physically active lifestyle. |
| NPH.K-12.4 Physical Fitness |
| Achieve and maintain a health-enhancing level of physical fitness. |
| NPH.K-12.6 Respect for Others |
| Demonstrate understanding and respect for differences among people in physical activity settings. |
| NPH.K-12.7 Understanding Challenge |
| Understand that physical activity provides opportunities for enjoyment, challenge, self-expression, and social interaction. |

# Chapter 4

# *Inquiry into Products People Make and Use*

## *Integrating Core Curriculum Content into Inquiry-Based Learning*

These units all have a hands-on, work-a-day focus. They ask questions about the world humans construct for utilitarian purposes—to live in a safe, warm house; to eat good food; to have products like paper for work and play; and to find our way around obstacles in nature because we have places to go and materials to transport. Thus, in addition to science and social studies, there is an element of practical, technical knowledge to be gained. These units take into account the real-life applications of scientific knowledge and acknowledge the role of industry and trades in our lives, elements that are not normally part of academic programs.

Each unit incorporates science education and social science core curriculum standards. The science education standards are based on national guidelines from the National Academies of Science and the American Association for the Advancement of Science. These standards are taken from the Education World® Web site. All standards met by the units that follow are listed at the end of the chapter.

## UNIT 1: *Building Homes*
### *(PreK to K)*

## A Good Choice for Inquiry

Children enjoy playing house, usually with pre-made kitchen play sets. This inquiry into how we build our homes will give them a deeper fund of knowledge to guide them at play. Exploring various places within a home builds vocabulary and curiosity about elements of their daily lives.

We all live somewhere and understand that we have basic needs that must be provided by our home. What does a plumber do in our home? Why do we have a basement in houses? How does heat get into our apartment? Once children have defined what is needed in a home, they can examine how those necessities are provided for, maintained, and changed.

## Background Reading

These books are written for adults but are highly visual and thus would make interesting resources for children once the inquiry is under way. Teachers will glean some specialized terminology and visual knowledge of homes that are found in their locality.

*American Homes: The Illustrated Encyclopedia of Domestic Architecture* by Les Walker (Black Dog & Leventhal, 2002)

*American Houses: A Field Guide to the Architecture of the Home* by Gerald L. Foster (Houghton Mifflin, 2004)

*The Visual Dictionary of American Domestic Architecture* by Rachel Carley (Holt, 1997)

## Unit Overview

An inquiry into how and why we build homes covers outcomes in science (scientific inquiry, technology, and personal and social perspectives). Social science goals related to environment are covered as well. By the end of the inquiry, students will:
- describe why people need homes
- describe the essential rooms in a house and the needs for each room
- identify and draw a particular type of home in their community
- describe their preferences for items in their own rooms at home
- describe their favorite room in their home and explain why they like it

## Guiding Questions

Why do we build our homes the way we do? What is needed in a home? What is just nice to have in a home?

## Specific Questions

- How do we build homes?
- What kind of homes do we have in our community?
- What kind of rooms do we have in our houses?
- What do we need to have in our homes?
- What do we like to have in our homes?
- How do we heat our homes?
- How do we keep our homes clean?
- Who makes repairs in our homes?
- How do human homes compare to animal homes?
- What different types of homes do people have in other parts of the world?
- How do you design a house?
- Can we design a playhouse?
- What are the jobs you need to do inside the house?
- How do you make your own room special inside your house?

## Controlled Vocabulary

- Architecture
- Building
- Domestic architecture
- Dwellings
- House construction
- For particular kinds of homes use Apartments, Houseboats, Houses, Mobile homes.

## Internet-Friendly Phrases

- "domestic architecture"
- "homes around the world"
- "how to build a house"

## Kid-Friendly Categories

Google Directory >      Kids and Teens
*Search within*          Pre-School > Houses and Homes
                              School Time > Social Studies > World Cultures

## Resources for *Building Homes*

### *Raise Interest and Stimulate Discussion*

*A Family for Old Mill Farm* by Shutta Crum, illustrated by Niki Daly (Clarion Books, 2007), proves to be a perfect home for both animals and human house-hunters.

*Homes* by Huan Yang, illustrated by Hsiao-yen Huang (Heryin Books, 2005), is a short, beautifully illustrated poem about how all creatures need a safe home.

*House Construction Ahead* [videorecording] (Fred Levine Productions, 2005) demonstrates how a house is built, from raw materials to the final touches.

*One Little Mouse* by Dori Chaconas (Viking, 2002) is a counting book about a mouse who believes he needs a new home.

*The Three Little Wolves and the Big Bad Pig* by Eugenios Trivizas, illustrated by Helen Oxenbury (Margaret K. McElderry Books, 1993), hilariously recounts the efforts of three harassed wolves as they try to build a house that will withstand the forceful attacks of pig.

### *Resource-Ready Core Collection*

*Apartment* by Lola M. Schaefer (Heinemann Library, 2003) looks at the function of rooms in an apartment.

*Building a House* by Byron Barton (Greenwillow Books, 1981) presents a simple, illustrated story of house construction.

*City and Country Homes* (Smart Apple Media, 2007) compares city and country houses around the world.

*A Day in the Life of a Builder* by Linda Hayward (DK Publishing, 2001) shows children what house builders do every day.

*A Day with a Bricklayer* by Mark Thomas, photographs by Maura Boruchow (Children's Press, 2001), shows a bricklayer named Nick at work.

*A Day with a Carpenter* by Joanne Winne, photographs by Maura Boruchow (Children's Press, 2001), follows a carpenter named John through typical jobs.

*A Day with an Electrician* by Mark Thomas, photographs by Maura Boruchow (Children's Press, 2001), follows an electrician named Peter as he does electrical jobs in people's homes.

*A Day with a Plumber* by Mark Thomas, photographs by Maura Boruchow (Children's Press, 2001), looks at the kinds of work that a plumber named Paul does for people in their homes.

*From Tree to House* [e-book] by Robin Nelson, photographs by Stephen G. Donaldson (Lerner Publications, 2004), is a simple, step-by-step description of house construction.

*Homes* by Margaret Hall (Heinemann Library, 2001) explains why people everywhere need homes.

*Homes* by Abby Jackson (Red Brick Learning, 2004) is an early reader about why people have homes.

*Homes* by Cassie Mayer (Heinemann Library, 2007) is an easy reader for emergent readers to try.

*Homes* by Emma Nathan (Blackbirch Press, 2002) shows how culture and geography influence the kind of house you live in.

*Homes for Everyone* by Jennifer B. Gillis (Rourke Publishing, 2007) looks at different types of homes.

*House* by Lola M. Schaefer (Heinemann Library, 2003) examines the variety of rooms needed in a house and includes a house map quiz.

*Houses* by Joanne Mattern, photographs by Richard Cummins (Smart Apple Media, 2003), explores the differences in design and materials used in houses.

*In My Home* by Mari C. Schuh (Pebble Books, 2006) features a young girl describing the different rooms in her house.

*Life at Home* by Vicki Yates (Heinemann Library, 2008) compares the elements in modern houses with those of yesteryear.

## Resource-Ready Supplementary Collection

*At Home: Long Ago and Today* by Lynnette R. Brent (Heinemann Library, 2003)

*Castle* by Dana Meachen Rau (Marshall Cavendish Benchmark, 2007)

*Cave and Underground Homes* by Debbie Gallagher (Smart Apple Media, 2007)

*City* by Peggy Pancella (Heinemann Library, 2006)

*A Day in the Life of a Construction Worker* by Heather Adamson (Capstone Press, 2004)

*Farm Community* by Peggy Pancella (Heinemann Library, 2006)

*A Farming Town* by Peter Roop (Heinemann Library, 1999)

*Home Then and Now* by Robin Nelson (Lerner Publications, 2003)

*Homes 1 2 3* by Lola M. Schaefer (Heinemann Library, 2003)

*Homes A B C* by Lola M. Schaefer (Heinemann Library, 2003)

*Homes around the World* by A. R. Schaefer (Rourke, 2007)

*Homes around the World ABC: An Alphabet Book* by Amanda Doering (Capstone Press, 2005)

*Homes* by Rosie McCormick (Smart Apple Media, 2004)

*Homes* by Kate Petty (Two-Can, 2006)

*Homes in Many Cultures* by Heather Adamson (Capstone Press, 2008)

*Homes on the Move* by Nicola Barber (Crabtree, 2008)

*Houseboat* by Lola M. Schaefer (Heinemann Library, 2003)

*Houses and Homes* by Ann Morris (Mulberry Books, 1994)

*I Live in a Town* [e-book] by Stasia Ward (PowerKids Press, 2000)

*I Want to Be a Builder* by Dan Liebman (Firefly Books, 2003)

*Igloo* by Dana Meachen Rau (Marshall Cavendish Benchmark, 2007)

*Living in a City* by Lisa Trumbauer (Capstone Press, 2005)

*Living in the Forest* by Donna Loughran (Children's Press, 2003)

*Living in a Rural Area* by Lisa Trumbauer (Capstone Press, 2005)

*Living in a Small Town* by Lisa Trumbauer (Capstone Press, 2005)

*Living in a Suburb* by Lisa Trumbauer (Capstone Press, 2005)

*Living near the Sea* by Allan Fowler (Children's Press, 2000)

*Log Cabin* by Dana Meachen Rau (Marshall Cavendish Benchmark, 2007)

*Mobile Home* by Lola M. Schaefer (Heinemann Library, 2003)

*Mud, Grass, and Ice Homes* by Debbie Gallagher (Smart Apple Media, 2007)

*Palaces, Mansions, and Castles* by Debbie Gallagher (Smart Apple Media, 2007)

*Portable Homes* by Debbie Gallagher (Smart Apple Media, 2007)

*Pueblos* by June Preszler (Capstone Press, 2005)

*River and Sea Homes* by Debbie Gallagher (Smart Apple Media, 2007)

*Skyscraper* by Dana Meachen Rau (Marshall Cavendish Benchmark, 2007)

*Small Town* by Peggy Pancella (Heinemann Library, 2006)

*Suburb* by Peggy Pancella (Heinemann Library, 2006)

*Tepee* by Dana Meachen Rau (Marshall Cavendish Benchmark, 2007)

*Tepees* by June Preszler (Capstone Press, 2005)

*Who's Who in a Public Housing Community* by Jake Miller (PowerKids Press, 2005)

*Who's Who in a Suburban Community* by Jake Miller (PowerKids Press, 2005)

*Wickiups* by June Preszler (Capstone Press, 2005)

## UNIT 2: Making Food Products
*(Grades 1 to 2)*

## A Good Choice for Inquiry

Everyone loves to eat, but many children at this age have had no hands-on experience with making food. Simple, delicious recipes for children will help build the confidence and motivation for those with no previous cooking experience. Children will find plenty of opportunity for sharing with their peers during this unit. Whether it is a discussion of favorite foods or what their parents cook, the subject never fails to inspire.

There are many attractive cookbooks in print for children. The most kid-friendly have been selected for the resource lists below. Children can compare what they cook themselves to the processes described by the many books about food products that are available for children in this age group. There is probably no better way to introduce nutrition concepts than with fun, hands-on cooking of real food.

## Background Reading

Teachers will want to think about suitable hands-on cooking and baking projects to support this inquiry. The cookbook listed here will get them started. Others are listed under the resource-ready collections. The second book is a handy reference to have if the children bring in boxes of processed foods. Teachers might wish to do a simple "kids cooking" search of You Tube <www.youtube.com> to look at examples of kids really cooking. Children find these much more engaging than watching an adult demonstrate how to cook.

*Cooking with Kids* by Sandra Rudloff (Bristol Publishing, 2000) provides recipes that adults and children can make together, including tips on cooking with young children.

*Food Labels: Using Nutrition Information to Create a Healthy Diet* by Rose McCarthy (Rosen Publishing, 2005) will help teachers analyze ingredients from processed foods.

## Unit Overview

An inquiry into making food products covers science goals related to scientific inquiry, life science, technology, personal and social perspectives, and the nature of science. Social studies outcomes include economic and environment goals. By the end of the inquiry students will:

- write a procedure for a recipe
- demonstrate a recipe and have it recorded on video
- explain the costs involved to produce their recipe
- identify the food groups of ingredients in their recipe
- assess the nutritional value of their recipe
- recount a story about cooking or food

## Guiding Questions

How do we make food at home and in factories? How do we mix ingredients to make food? How are ingredients changed when we make food?

## Specific Questions

- What can we make to eat?
- How does food change when we cook?
- What foods are made in factories?
- What kinds of ingredients go into foods?
- What is a healthy food?
- Why do people eat different foods?
- Why are some people vegetarians?
- What foods are people allergic to?
- What can we find out from food labels?
- What are the rules about packaging foods?
- How long do packaged foods last?
- What food can I learn to make?
- What is safe for me to learn to make?
- How is packaged food different from home-cooked food?
- What is the difference between the way we make bread at home and the way bakers make bread at a bakery?

## Controlled Vocabulary

- Baking
- Cookery
- Food
- For particular kinds of food products use Applesauce, Bread, Cheese.

## Internet-Friendly Phrases

- "baking bread"
- "making chocolate from cocoa beans"
- "making an omelet"
- "making a smoothie"

## Kid-Friendly Categories

| | |
|---|---|
| Google Directory > | Kids and Teens |
| *Search within* | Sports and Hobbies > Cooking |
| | Sports and Hobbies > Cooking > Ethnic |
| | School Time > Social Studies > World Cultures |

# Resources for *Making Food Products*

## *Raise Interest and Stimulate Discussion*

*Chicks and Salsa* by Aaron Reynolds, illustrated by Paulette Bogan (Bloomsbury Children's Books, 2005), is a funny tale of barnyard animals trying to rustle up something tastier than the usual fare.

*Eight Animals Bake a Cake* by Susan Middleton Elya, illustrated by Lee Chapman (Putnam, 2002), is a funny look at cooking together that will get kids talking about cooperation.

*Fairy Tale Feasts: A Literary Cookbook for Young Readers and Eaters: Fairy Tales* Retold by Jane Yolen, recipes by Heidi E. Y. Stemple, illustrated by Philippe Beha (Crocodile Books, 2006), is a pairing of well-told fairy tales with related recipes.

*Feast for 10* by Cathryn Falwell (Clarion Books, 1993) is a counting story about a family who shops for food and prepares a meal together.

*Henry and Mudge and the Funny Lunch* by Cynthia Rylant, illustrated by Carolyn Bracken in the style of Sucie Stevenson (Simon & Schuster Books for Young Readers, 2004), feature Henry and his dad as they come up with some amusing food treats for his mom on Mother's Day.

*How to Make an Apple Pie and See the World* by Marjorie Priceman (A. Knopf, 1994) is a wacky story of a girl who finds the market closed, so she sets off to buy ingredients for her apple pie from their original setting (cinnamon from Sri Lanka, wheat from Italy).

*Kids Get Cooking: Eggs* [videorecording] (Goldhil Entertainment, 2005) features kids cooking and learning about eggs.

*The Princess and the Pizza* by Mary Jane Auch, illustrated by Herm Auch (Holiday House, 2002), tells the story of a princess who tries to impress Prince Drupert with her cooking, but opts for her own pizza restaurant in the end.

## *Resource-Ready Core Collection*

*Berries to Jelly* by Inez Snyder (Children's Press, 2005) uses simple text to describe the process step-by-step.

*Cereal* by Gretchen Mayo (Weekly Reader Early Learning Library, 2004) takes cereal from the field to the breakfast bowl.

*The Edible Pyramid: Good Eating Every Day* by Loreen Leedy (Holiday House, 2007) is based on the new Department of Agriculture's food pyramid but set in the fun animal-filled Edible Pyramid restaurant.

*Follow that Food* by Buffy Silverman (Raintree, 2007) looks at the ingredients in the ever-popular pepperoni pizza, tracing each ingredient from their origin to how they are processed.

*First Facts: From Farm to Table* series by Kristin Thoennes Keller (Capstone Press, 2005) offers 10 clearly written guides to food production: *From Apples to Applesauce, From Cane to Sugar, From Corn to Cereal, From Maple Trees to Maple Syrup, From Milk to Cheese, From Milk to Ice Cream, From Oranges to Orange Juice, From Peanuts to Peanut Butter, From Tomato to Ketchup,* and *From Wheat to Bread.*

*First Step Nonfiction: Food Groups* series [e-books] by Robin Nelson (Lerner, 2003) includes six titles that present various foods in the groups of the food pyramid: Dairy; Fats, Oils, and Sweets; Fruits; Grains; Meats and Proteins; and Vegetables.

*Plants as Food* by Paul McEvoy (Chelsea Clubhouse, 2003) makes the case that plants provide all our food, either directly or indirectly.

*Pretend Soup and Other Real Recipes: A Cookbook for Preschoolers & Up* by Mollie Katzen and Ann Henderson, illustrated by Mollie Katzen (Tricycle Press, 1994), is written by a cookbook writer and an educator specifically for preschoolers and the adults who want them to enjoy the process of cooking.

*Salad People and More Real Recipes: A New Cookbook for Preschoolers & Up* by Mollie Katzen (Tricycle Press, 2005) has recipes in print for the adults and in picture format for the kids. This volume presents 20 vegetarian dishes.

*Sap to Syrup* by Inez Snyder (Children's Press, 2005) is another simple step-by-step guide.

*The Science Chef: 100 Fun Food Experiments and Recipes for Kids* by Joan D'Amico and Karen Eich Drummond, illustrated by Tina Cash-Walsh (J. Wiley, 1995)

*Where Does Our Food Come From?* series by Gretchen Mayo (Weekly Reader Early Learning Library, 2004) explains how common foods are processed: Applesauce, Cereal, Frozen Vegetables, Milk, Orange Juice, and Pasta.

## Resource-Ready Supplementary Collection

*The Baking Book* by Jane Bull (DK Publishing, 2005)

*The Cooking Book* by Jane Bull (DK Publishing, 2002)

*Food and Recipes of Africa* [e-book] by Theresa M. Beatty (Rosen Publishing, 1999)

*Food and Recipes of the Caribbean* [e-book] by Theresa M. Beatty (PowerKids Press, 1999)

*Food and Recipes of China* [e-book] by Theresa M. Beatty (Rosen Publishing, 1999)

*Food and Recipes of Greece* [e-book] by Theresa M. Beatty (PowerKids Press, 1999)

*Food and Recipes of Japan* [e-book] by Theresa M. Beatty (Rosen Publishing, 1999)

*Food and Recipes of Mexico* [e-book] by Theresa M. Beatty (PowerKids Press, 1999)

*Fruits* by Emily K. Green (Bellwether Media, 2007)

*Grains* by Emily K. Green (Bellwether Media, 2007)

*Healthy Eating* by Emily K. Green (Bellwether Media, 2007)

*Holy Guacamole!: And Other Scrumptious Snacks* by Nick Fauchald, illustrated by Rick Peterson (Picture Window Books, 2008)

*How Is Chocolate Made?* by Angela Royston (Heinemann Library, 2005)

*How It Happens at the Candy Company* by Jenna Anderson, photographs by Bob and Diane Wolfe (Clara House Books, 2002)

*Kids Cook 1-2-3: Recipes for Young Chefs Using Only 3 Ingredients* by Rozanne Gold, illustrated by Sara Pinto (Bloomsbury Children's Books, 2006)

*Meat and Beans* by Emily K. Green (Bellwether Media, 2007)

*Milk, Yogurt, and Cheese* by Emily K. Green (Bellwether Media, 2007)

*Oils* by Emily K. Green (Bellwether Media, 2007)

*The Usborne First Cookbook* by Angela Wilkes, illustrated by Stephen Cartwright (Esborne, 2006)

*Vegetables* by Emily K. Green (Bellwether Media, 2007)

**UNIT 2: *Making Food Products***

## UNIT 3: *Making Paper*
*(Grades 3 to 4)*

## A Good Choice for Inquiry

Every school can provide hands-on inquiry on this topic. We all use paper every day and try to recycle. Kids can investigate just what is happening to waste paper at their own school. Even if paper plants are not available in the local vicinity, recycling centers often are. For those without access to either, online presentations are interactive, with interesting animations and sound. Making paper oneself is an easy process requiring ordinary kitchen implements. For those who wish to experiment, there is scope for creative variations. Even the old wasp's nest in the eave of the school roof can become part of the investigation. Any way you look at it, making paper and recycling paper is a part of all of our lives.

There is a good variety of resources to support this inquiry. Interactive sites are useful for opening the inquiry as a class, using an interactive whiteboard. Printable colored posters can provide models for the classroom. Fictionalized accounts of the invention of paper may even inspire other accounts. Artistic types might experiment with handmade paper projects. Mathematical types might look at the costs involved in recycling—and not recycling. There is truly something for everyone in an inquiry into making paper.

## Background Reading

*The Paper Project: A New Light on Paper* <http://paperproject.org/> takes a scientific yet accessible approach to the ancient technology and art of papermaking.

*The Papermaker's Companion: The Ultimate Guide to Making and Using Handmade Paper* by Helen Hiebert (Storey Books, 2000) is a good basic manual with detailed instructions.

*Recycling Poster* <www.paperrecycles.org/recycling/school/Recycling_poster.pdf> is a two-page downloadable poster and brochure giving a short, colorful guide to all aspects of recycling, industrial papermaking, and home papermaking. Written for educators.

*Tools for Teachers: Paper Industry Association Council (PIAC)* <www.paperrecycles.org/tools_for_teachers/index.html> offers many resources for teachers, statistics on paper recycling, and kid-friendly videos.

## Unit Overview

An inquiry into how paper is made covers science outcomes related to scientific inquiry, life science, technology, personal and social perspectives, and the nature of science. Social science outcomes include geography and economic content. By the end of the inquiry, students will:

■ present simple bar graphs showing what they have learned about paper use at school
■ explain the procedure to follow to make handmade paper
■ use a diagram to explain the steps to make paper in a factory
■ use Venn diagrams to compare aspects of papermaking in a factory and at home
■ recall and retell stories about papermaking

## Guiding Questions

How is paper made in industrial plants and at home? Where and how does recycling come into play?

## Specific Questions

■ What are the steps to making paper in a factory?
■ What is a pulp and paper plant? How is it different from a paper mill?
■ What are the steps to making paper at home?
■ What are the main ingredients of paper made in a factory?
■ What are the main ingredients of paper made at home?
■ Can ingredients vary in both situations?
■ What does it cost to produce paper in a factory?
■ What does it cost to produce paper at home?
■ How does recycling affect the cost of paper?
■ How much energy does it take to produce paper in a factory?
■ How much energy does it take to produce paper at home?
■ How much paper do we use at school?
■ What do we use paper for at school?
■ Do we use different kinds of paper at school?
■ What is cost of the different kinds of paper that we use at school?
■ How much paper do we recycle at school?
■ Where does our recycled paper go?
■ What is the recycled content of the paper we use at school?
■ Is a wasp nest really made of paper?

## Controlled Vocabulary

■ Paper
■ Papermaking
■ Paper products
■ Paper wasps
■ Recycling (Waste)
■ Waste products

# Internet-Friendly Phrases

- "paper recycling"
- "papermaking"
- "paper wasp"

# Kid-Friendly Categories

Google Directory >    Kids and Teens
*Search within*    School Time > Science
    School Time > Science > Environment

# Resources for *Making Paper*

## Raise Interest and Stimulate Discussion

*The Cloudmakers* by James Rumford (Houghton Mifflin, 1996) is an adventure tale of kidnapping, negotiation, and papermaking.

*The Story of Paper* by Ying Chang Compestine, illustrated by YongSheng Xuan (Holiday House, 2003), features the clever Kang brothers who invent paper as a way to stop their teacher from writing notes on their hands. The story concludes with a factual note from the author and directions for making homemade paper.

## Resource-Ready Core Collection

*The Blue Cart Program* <http://egov.cityofchicago.org/city/webportal/home.do> of the
    City of Chicago has replaced blue bags with blue carts. This simpler approach to
    recycling allows all recyclables to be placed together. Follow links to Streets and
    Sanitation > Chicago Recycling Initiatives.
*Bluewater Recycling Association* <www.bra.org/virtual.html> presents an easy-to-follow
    photo album of the material recovery facility in Huron Park, Ontario.
*City Carton Recycling: How We Do It* <www.citycarton.com/index_files/CityCarton
    RecyclingHowWeDoIt.htm> is another simple photo essay on a recycling center.
    From Tree to Paper by Pam Marshall (Lerner, 2003) follows the papermaking process
    from start to finish.
*How Bowater Makes Paper* <http://www.bowater.com/flash/makingpaper.swf> is a flash
    presentation of the industrial papermaking process led by "Chip," the Bowater
    wood chipper.
*How We Use Paper* by Chris Oxlade (Raintree, 2005) covers the different kinds of paper
    and its uses in short, clear sentences.
*Open a Newspaper* by Susan Korman (Blackbirch Press, 2004) shows how newspapers are
    created and used.

*Paper* by Alexandra Fix (Heinemann Library, 2008) is a simple introduction to all aspects of paper recycling.

*A Paper Bag* by Sue Barraclough (Gareth Stevens Publishing, 2005) looks at each step in the process of making a paper bag–from the trees to the mill, the factory, and finally, the retail shop.

*Paper (Reading Essentials in Science: How Things are Made)* by Beth Dvergsten Stevens (Perfection Learning, 2004) looks at the history of paper and how it is made today.

*Paper (Recycling and Reusing)* by Ruth Thomson (Smart Apple Media, 2006) examines the many options for reusing paper, including handmade paper.

*Paper University* <www.tappi.org/paperu/welcome.htm> has detailed but accessible interactive and step-by-step guides to the process of industrial and home papermaking, plus many related topics including recycling and forestry.

*Paper Wasp (Bug Books series)* by Monica Harris (Heinemann Library, 2003) explores all aspects of these wasps and their paper-making cells, using compelling photographs and simple text.

*Papermaking (Step by Step)* by David Watson (Heinemann, 2000)

*Papermaking for Kids: Simple Steps to Handcrafted Paper* by Beth Wilkinson and Albert Molnar (Gibbs Smith Publishers, 1997)

*Papermaking Process* <http://www.ppic.org.uk/info/process/process.htm> is a clickable image map of the entire industrial papermaking process, using clear illustrations and photographs.

*A Tour of the Material Recovery Facility* <http://gocolumbiamo.com/PublicWorks/Solidwaste/flash/mrf_tour.swf> gives photos, text, and diagrams of the City of Columbia's material recovery center, lead by mascot Mr. Bag-It!

*Trees to Paper* by Inez Snyder (Children's Press, 2003) is a high-interest, low-reading book on the industrial process of paper making.

## Resource-Ready Supplementary Collection

*Paper* by Helen Bliss (Crabtree, 1998)

*Paper* by Sara Louise Kras (Capstone Press, 2004)

*Paper* by Claire Llewellyn (Sea-to-Sea, 2006)

*Paper* by Holly Wallace (Smart Apple Media, 2008)

*Paper* (Recycle, Reduce, Reuse, Rethink) by Kate Walker (Smart Apple Media, 2004)

*Recycling Materials* by Sue Barraclough (Sea-to-Sea, 2008)

*Recycling Paper (Just Rubbish)* by Judith Condon, illustrated by Maggie Murray (Franklin Watts, 1990)

*Trash and Recycling: Paper Making, Kid Kit* by Stephanie Turnbull, illustrated by Christyan Fox (Usborne Books, 2007)

## UNIT 4: *Building Bridges*
*(Grades 5 to 6)*

## A Good Choice for Inquiry

Building bridges is a popular topic in the upper elementary and middle years. It is easy to incorporate math and science concepts, with some history and geography elements to give the theme wide appeal. Many skills are necessary for this model-building project, making it a good unit for group work and sharing of various strengths among students. This, in turn, increases individual student motivation. A model-building project does not imply competition. Students who are not naturally disposed to engineering and design can select simple models and simpler design principles, yet still achieve success.

There is a plethora of material available for this project. Highly interactive online sites help children investigate physical forces and real-life bridge-building without having to don a hardhat. Videos and photographs of modern superstructures impress young minds and stimulate interest in this topic. Stories are available as well for those who prefer information in a narrative format.

## Background Reading

*Building Toothpick Bridges* by Jeanne Pollard (Dale Seymour Publications, 1985) is a professional resource that focuses on the math content of a model-building project for children in grades 5 through 8.

*Super Bridge* [videorecording] (WGBH, 1997) allows the viewer to experience firsthand the entire process of a four-year bridge-building project in this two-hour special from the NOVA series on PBS.

## Unit Overview

An inquiry into bridges covers science in terms of scientific inquiry, physical science, science and technology, personal and social perspectives, and the history and nature of science. Social science outcomes include economic, geography, and history content standards. By the end of the inquiry, students will:

■ describe the planning, building, and testing of their model bridge
■ describe the forces at work when an object travels across their model bridge
■ describe places and circumstances where their bridge would be a good choice over other
■ types of bridges
■ compare their bridge to another type of bridge

## Guiding Questions

How can we build a good working model of a bridge?

## Specific Questions

- What materials should we use?
- How strong can we make our bridge?
- What type of bridge should we build?
- How can we test the strength of our bridge?
- Why do some bridges collapse?
- What does an engineer have to know to design a good bridge?
- How do we monitor the safety of bridges in our community?
- How much does it cost to build a bridge?
- How long does it take to build a bridge?
- How long do bridges last?

## Controlled Vocabulary

- Bridges
- Bridges design and construction
- Building materials
- Civil engineering
- Civil engineers
- Models and model making
- Structural analysis (Engineering)
- Structural engineering
- For particular bridges use Akashi Kaikyo Bridge (Kobe-shi, Japan).

## Internet-Friendly Phrases

- "bridge building"
- "famous bridges"
- "types of bridges"

## Kid-Friendly Categories

Google Directory > Kids and Teens

Search within    School Time > Science > Technology > Building and Bridges
                 (includes category Model Bridge Building)

# Resources for *Building Bridges*

## *Raise Interest and Stimulate Discussion*

*The 10 Most Amazing Bridges* by Suzanne Harper (Franklin Watts, 2008) will draw students to the inspiring characteristics of bridges.

*Bridges: From My Side to Yours* by Jan Adkins (Roaring Brook Press, 2002) uses narrative and illustrations to stimulate interest in bridges. Fascinating and horrifying by turns, it will draw students to this theme.

*Bridges Are to Cross* by Philemon Sturges (G.P. Putnam's Sons, 1998) has detailed illustrations that will attract student interest and keep them exploring.

*Building Big* by David Macaulay (Houghton Mifflin, 2000) offers his usual lucid and highly visual treatment of architectural feats. A videorecording (WGBH Boston Video, 2000) with the same title makes a good companion to stimulate classroom discussion.

*Brooklyn Bridge* by Lynn Curlee (Atheneum Books for Young Readers, 2001) tells the fascinating 16-year history of the building of this bridge and is sure to stimulate ideas for further investigation.

*The Great Bridge-Building Contest* by Bo Zaunders, illustrated by Roxie Munro (Harry N. Abrams, 2004), would make an excellent read-aloud to stimulate interest. It tells how Lemuel Chenoweth, an uneducated cabinetmaker, beat trained engineers to build a bridge across the Tygart River. The scene where Chenoweth sets his model between two chairs and walks across it is sure to surprise.

## *Resource-Ready Core Collection*

*Bridges!: Amazing Structures to Design, Build & Test* (Kaleidoscope Kids series) by Carol Johmann and Elizabeth Rieth, illustrated by Michael Kline (Williamson, 1999), has commendable range: it covers the science, history and how-to of bridges, and includes examples from the United States (state-by-state), Canada (province-by-province), and internationally (country-by-country).

*Bridges* (True Books series) by Elaine Landau (Children's Press, 2001) is a basic resource covering history, construction, and types of bridges.

*Bridges* (Building Amazing Structures) by Chris Oxlade, illustrations by Barry Atkinson (Heinemann Library, 2006), focuses on the design, construction, and maintenance of bridges.

*Bridge Basics: A Spotter's Guide to Bridge Design* <pghbridges.com/basics.htm> presents simple, clear diagrams of bridge designs.

*Bridge Building: Bridge Designs and How They Work* by Diane Briscoe (Red Brick Learning, 2005) looks at bridge design principles from ancient Rome to the present, including some disastrous failures.

*Building Big: Bridge Basics* <www.pbs.org/wgbh/buildingbig/bridge/basics.html> from PBS is a well-designed, interactive look at the design principles of various types of bridges.

*Engineering the City: How Infrastructure Works: Projects and Principles for Beginners* by Matthys Levy and Richard Panchyk (Chicago Review Press, 2000) will appeal to students who already are attracted to math and engineering.

*Fantastic Feats and Failures* by the editors of Yes Mag (Kids Can Press, 2004) examines successes and failures in particular buildings, bridges, and dams.

*I Wonder Why Tunnels are Round: And Other Questions about Building* by Steve Parker (Kingfisher, 1995) will help children find unusual questions about bridges.

*Matsuo Bridge: Bridges: The Basic Bridge Types* <http://www.matsuo-bridge.co.jp/english/bridges/index.shtm> has clear diagrams and gives a brief rationale for materials and design of the six types of bridges presented.

*Steven Caney's Ultimate Building Book* by Steven Caney (Running Press Kids, 2006) offers thought-provoking information on materials and construction.

*Super Bridge: Build a Bridge* <www.pbs.org/wgbh/nova/bridge/build.html> is a fun, accessible site. It includes hands-on tests of bridge types using simple materials such as string, hard cover books, and the students' own arms to teach about forces. It concludes with an interactive, practical test of their new knowledge.

## Resource-Ready Supplementary Collection

*The Akashi Kaikyo Bridge: World's Longest Bridge* by Mark Thomas (PowerKids Press, 2002)

*American Indian Contributions to the World: Trade, Transportation, and Warfare* by Emory Dean Keoke (Facts on File, 2005)

*The Art of Construction: Projects and Principles for Beginning Engineers and Architects* by Mario George Salvadori, illustrated by Saralinda Hooker and Christopher Ragus (Chicago Review Press, 1990)

*Building* (Make It Work! Science series) by Andrew Haslam and David Glover, illustrated by Jon Barnes (Two-Can, 1994)

*Built to Last: Building America's Amazing Bridges, Dams, Tunnels, and Skyscrapers* by George Sullivan (Scholastic Nonfiction, 2005)

*Construction Math* (Math and My World series) by Kieran Walsh (Rourke Publishing, 2006)

*Extreme Structures: Mega-Construction of the 21st Century* (Science Frontiers) by David Jefferis (Crabtree Publishing, 2006)

*Famous Bridges of the World: Measuring Length, Weight, and Volume* by Yolonda Maxwell (PowerKids Press, 2005)

*The Golden Gate Bridge* by Sharlene P. Nelson (Children's Press, 2001)

*The Longest Bridge* by Darv Johnson (Kidhaven Press, 2003)

*The Longest Bridges* by Susan K. Mitchell (Gareth Stevens Publishing, 2008)

*The Royal Gorge Bridge* by Margaret Speaker-Yuan (Blackbirch Press, 2004)

*What's That?: A Field Guide to Technology* by Edwin J. C. Sobey (Franklin Watts, 2003)

## Figure 4.1  Standards for Unit 1—*Building Homes*

| **Science** |
| --- |
| NS.K-4.1 Science as Inquiry |
| Develop abilities necessary to do scientific inquiry. |
| Develop understandings about scientific inquiry. |
| NS.K-4.5 Science and Technology |
| Develop understandings about science and technology. |
| NS.K-4.6 Personal and Social Perspectives |
| Develop understanding of types of resources. |
| Develop understanding of changes in environments. |
| Develop understanding of science and technology in local challenges. |
| NS.K-4.7 History and Nature of Science |
| Develop understanding of science as a human endeavor. |
| **Social Science** |
| NSS-EC.K-4.7 Markets |
| A price is what people pay when they buy a good or service. |
| NSS-G.K-12.5 Environment and Society |
| Understand how human actions modify the physical environment. |
| Understand the changes that occur in the meaning, use, distribution, and importance of resources. |

## Figure 4.2  Standards for Unit 2—*Making Food Products*

| Science |
|---|
| NS.K-4.1 Science as Inquiry |
| Develop abilities necessary to do scientific inquiry. |
| Develop understandings about scientific inquiry. |
| NS.K-4.3 Life Science |
| Develop an understanding of life cycles of organisms. |
| Develop an understanding of organisms and environments. |
| NS.K-4.5 Science and Technology |
| Develop understandings about science and technology. |
| NS.K-4.6 Personal and Social Perspectives |
| Develop understanding of types of resources. |
| NS.K-4.7 History and Nature of Science |
| Develop understanding of science as a human endeavor. |

| Social Science |
|---|
| NSS-EC.K-4.7 Markets |
| A price is what people pay when they buy a good or service. |
| NSS-G.K-12.5 Environment and Society |
| Understand how human actions modify the physical environment. |
| Understand the changes that occur in the meaning, use, distribution, and importance of resources. |

## Figure 4.3  Standard for Units 3—*Making Paper*

| Science |
|---|
| NS.K-4.1 Science as Inquiry |
| Develop abilities necessary to do scientific inquiry. |
| Develop understandings about scientific inquiry. |
| NS.K-4.3 Life Science |
| Develop an understanding of the characteristics of organisms. |
| Develop an understanding of life cycles of organisms. |
| Develop an understanding of organisms and environments. |
| NS.K-4.5 Science and Technology |
| Develop understandings about science and technology. |
| NS.K-4.6 Personal and Social Perspectives |
| Develop understanding of types of resources. |
| Develop understanding of changes in environments. |
| Develop understanding of science and technology in local challenges. |
| NS.K-4.7 History and Nature of Science |
| Develop understanding of science as a human endeavor. |

| Social Science |
|---|
| NSS-EC.K-4.7 Markets |
| A price is what people pay when they buy a good or service. |
| NSS-G.K-12.1 The World in Spatial Terms |
| Understand how to use maps and other geographic representations. |
| NSS-G.K-12.5 Environment and Society |
| Understand how human actions modify the physical environment. |
| Understand the changes that occur in the meaning, use, distribution, and importance of resources. |

## Figure 4.4  Standards for Unit 4—*Building Bridges*

| Science |
|---|
| NS.5-8.1 Science as Inquiry |
| Develop abilities necessary to do scientific inquiry. |
| Develop understandings about scientific inquiry. |
| NS.5-8.2 Physical Science |
| Develop an understanding of motions and forces. |
| NS.5-8.5 Science and Technology |
| Develop abilities of technological design. |
| Develop understandings about science and technology. |
| NS.5-8.6 Science and Social Perspectives |
| Develop understanding of populations, resources, and environments. |
| Develop understanding of natural hazards. |
| Develop understanding of risks and benefits. |
| Develop understanding of science and technology in society. |
| NS.5-8.7 History and Nature of Science |
| Develop understanding of science as a human endeavor. |
| Develop understanding of the nature of science. |
| Develop understanding of the history of science. |

| Social Science |
|---|
| NSS-EC.5-8.1 Scarcity |
| The choices people make have both present and future consequences. |
| NSS-G.K-12.1 The World in Spatial Terms |
| Understand how to use maps and other geographic representations. |
| NSS-G.K-12.5 Environment and Society |
| Understand how human actions modify the physical environment. |
| Understand how physical systems affect human systems. |

# Chapter 5

# *Inquiry into Our Community*

## *Integrating Core Curriculum Content into Inquiry-Based Learning*

Stories help children to understand their world. Storytelling is an engaging and creative way to approach information themes and projects. In these units, very young children share stories about those closest to them—family and friends. Middle grade students use language to both inform and persuade. Older kids compose news stories to report about their classroom work and news to the wider school community. In all instances, language is the focus as children use different writing and speaking styles to convey a message to a specific audience.

Each unit focuses on achieving language arts standards. These standards are derived from the NCTE (National Council of Teachers of English). They appear in full on Education World®'s Web site. All standards met by the units that follow are listed at the end of the chapter.

*Families*
*(PreK to K)*

## A Good Choice for Inquiry

At this age, family is important. Children enjoy talking about their parents, brothers, sisters, cousins, and grandparents. They notice differences between families as their classmates arrive at school. It is important for them to have a chance to explore the many ways that families exist and support one another.

## Background Reading

This is a common theme in preschool and kindergarten. Teachers are likely to feel comfortable with the topic and probably have covered it in previous years. One of the few unfamiliar questions that may arise, however, is how people adopt children, both domestically and internationally. Stories about adoption are included in the resource lists. The following background reading may help.

*The Adoption Guide* <www.theadoptionguide.com> is a Web site copyrighted to Adoptive Families magazine. It contains general guidelines for prospective adopters.

*The Ultimate Insider's Guide to Adoption: Everything You need to Know about Domestic and International Adoption* by Elizabeth Swire Falker (Warner Wellness, 2006) is up-to-date and comprehensive.

## Unit Overview

An inquiry into families covers language arts curriculum standards. By the end of the inquiry, students will:

■ produce a simple family tree of their immediate family, with photos or drawings and labels
■ describe the variety of families in the class
■ develop a chart together comparing family size for all families in the class
■ produce a simple story about what they enjoy doing with their family

## Guiding Questions

What can we tell others about our family and other families in our community?

## Specific Questions

- What are families like?
- How big are families in our community?
- Where do our families come from?
- Where do our families live?
- When do we see our families?
- Who is in our family?
- What do we like to do together as a family?

## Controlled Vocabulary

- Family

## Internet-Friendly Phrases

- "foster families"
- "family members"

## Kid-Friendly Categories

Google Directory >      Kids and Teens
*Search within*         Preschool > People > My Family
                        Preschool > People > Babies
                        Your Family

## Resources for *Families*

### *Raise Interest and Stimulate Discussion*

*All for Pie, Pie for All* by David Martin, illustrated by Valeri Gorbachev (Candlewick Press, 2006), shows a cat family sharing with mice and ants.

*The Best Single Mom in the World: How I Was Adopted* by Mary Zisk (A. Whitman, 2001)

*Families* by Susan Kuklin (Hyperion Books for Children, 2006) use the interviews by kids to stimulate interest—children were allowed to direct the production of this book—an excellent exemplar of a potential final product.

*Families Are Different* by Nina Pellegrini (Holiday House, 1991) explores the many types of families today.

*A Father Like That* by Charlotte Zolotow, illustrated by LeUyen Pham (HarperCollins, 2007), looks at a single-parent family.

*Mama, I'll Give You the World* by Roni Schotter, illustrated by S. Saelig Gallagher (Schwartz & Wade Books, 2006)

*Mommy's Briefcase* by Alice Low, illustrated by Aliki (Scholastic, 1995)

*The Red Blanket* by Eliza Thomas, illustrated by Joe Cepeda (Scholastic, 2004), treats international adoption by single parents.

## Resource-Ready Core Collection

*Aunts* by Lola M. Schaefer (Capstone Press, 2008)

*Baby on the Way* by William Sears and Christie Watts Kelly, illustrated by Renee Andriani (Little, Brown, 2001)

*Brothers* by Lola M. Schaefer (Capstone Press, 2008)

*Catherine and Laurence Anholt's Big Book of Families* by Catherine Anholt and Laurence Anholt (Candlewick, 1998)

*Families (Our Global Community)* by Lisa Easterling (Heinemann Library, 2007)

*Families* by Susan Kuklin (Hyperion Books for Children, 2006)

*Families* by Ann Morris (HarperCollins, 2000)

*Families* by Meredith Tax, illustrated by Marylin Hafner (The Feminist Press at the City University of New York, 1996)

*The Family Book* by Todd Parr (Little, Brown, 2003)

*A Family Like Yours* by Rebecca Kai Dotlich, illustrated by Tammie Lyon (Wordsong/Boyds Mills Press, 2002)

*Family Pets* by Lola M. Schaefer (Capstone Press, 2008)

*Fathers* by Lola M. Schaefer (Capsone Press, 2008)

*How My Family Lives in America* by Susan Kuklin (Aladdin Paperbacks, 1998)

*Love that Baby!: A Book about Babies for New Brothers, Sisters, Cousins and Friends* by Kathrun Lasky (Candlewick Press, 2004)

*My Family* by Sheila Kinkade, photographs by Elaine Little (Shakti for Children Charlesbridge, 1006)

*We Belong Together: A Book about Adoption and Families* by Todd Parr (Little, Brown, 2007)

*What is a Family?* by Craig Hammersmith, illustrated by Anna-Maria Crum (Compass Point Books, 2003)

## Resource-Ready Supplementary Collection

*All about Adoption: How Families Are Made & How Kids Feel about It* by Marc. A. Nemiroff (Magination Press, 2004)

*All Families are Different* by Sol Gordon, illustrated by Viven Cohen (Prometheus Books, 2000)

*Apache Children and Elders Talk Together* by E. Barrie Kavasch (PowerKids Press, 1999)

*Dinosaurs Divorce: A Guide for Changing Families* by Laurene Krasny Brown (Little, Brown, 1986)

*Families* by Debbie Bailey, photographs by Susan Huszar (Annick Press, 1999)

*Families* by Gail Saunders-Smith (Pebble Books, 1998)

*Families* by Lisa Trumbauer (Yellow Umbrella Books, 2001)

*Families Change: A Book for Children Experiencing Termination of Parental Rights* by Julie Nelson, illustrated by Mary Gallagher (Free Spirit Publishing, 2007)

*Families Have Together* by Harriet Ziefert, illustrated by Deborah Zemke (Blue Apple Books, 2005)

*Families: Poems Celebrating the African American Experience* by Dorothy S. Strickland and Michael R. Strickland, illustrations by John Ward (Wordsong/Boyds Mills Press, 1994)

*Grandfathers* by Lola M. Schaefer (Capstone Press, 2008)

*Let's Talk about Adoption* by Diana Star Helmer (PowerKids Press, 1999)

*Let's Talk about Living with a Single Parent* by Elizabeth Weitzman (PowerKids Press, 1996)

*Let's Talk about Living with Your Single Dad* by Melanie Ann Apel (PowerKids Press, 2001)

*Mothers* by Lola M. Schaefer (Capstone Press, 2008)

*Sisters* by Lola M. Schaefer (Capstone Press, 2008)

*Uncles* by Lola M. Schaefer (Capstone Press, 2008)

## UNIT 2: *Friends*
*(Grades 1 to 2)*

## A Good Choice for Inquiry

Books that explain how to get along with friends can be preachy or simplistic. Stories about friendship have much more appeal for children. In fact, there are so many storybooks about friendship written for children of this age that any library is sure to have loads of resources already. Have the children explore the shelves, hunting for good friendship books. The resources listed here are recently published or easy readers that children of this age can enjoy on their own.

Approached as a storytelling unit, children can be given a lot of freedom to choose how they wish to proceed. Everyone loves a good story, and building storytelling skills in children helps them to become better readers as well.

## Background Reading

Most teachers are very familiar with the theme of friendship in the early elementary years. They probably will not need background reading other than a good selection of friendship stories, as listed below in the resource-ready section. The Web site below may help them introduce the topic with children during classroom discussion.

*Kids' Health: Topics: Friendship* <http://cyh.com/HealthTopics/HealthTopicDetailsKids. aspx?p=335&np=286&id=1636#5> gives examples of what other school children are writing and drawing about friends.

## Unit Overview

An inquiry into friends covers language arts standards. By the end of this inquiry, students will:
- recount a story about friendship
- present a list of the qualities they look for in a friend in an artistic and engaging way
- write a story about fictional friends who resolve a problem together

## Guiding Questions

What do we look for in a friend? What stories can we tell about friends?

## Specific Questions

- How do we make friends?
- What do friends do together?
- How can we stop bullying?
- Why do we need friends?

- What can we do when friends move away?
- How can I be a good friend?
- What words do we use to describe friends and friendship?
- What special qualities do we personally look for in a friend?
- How do we resolve conflicts with our friends?
- What can we do to show our friends that we care?
- Can we tell stories about our friends?
- Can we create a fictional story about friends?

## Controlled Vocabulary

- Behavior
- Best friends
- Bossiness
- Friends
- Friendship
- Interpersonal relations
- Jealousy
- Secrets
- To find stories add Fiction

## Internet-Friendly Phrases

- "conflict resolution"
- "stop bullying"

## Kid-Friendly Categories

Google Directory >     Kids and Teens
*Search within*            Health > Emotional Health and Well-being
                              Health > Emotional Health and Well-being > Bullying

## Resources for *Friends*

### *Raise Interest and Stimulate Discussion*

*Cookies: Bite-Size Life Lessons* by Amy Krouse Rosenthal, illustrated by Jane Dyer (HarperCollins, 2006), received starred reviews for the original and lifelike way it deals with terms such as cooperate, patient, respect, regret, and trustworthy. A good vocabulary builder for this unit that would pair up well with *The Little Red Hen Makes a Pizza.*

*The Friendly Four* by Eloise Greenfield, illustrated by Jan Spivey Gilchrist (HarperCollins, 2006), is a collection of free-verse poems about an appealing group of kids who meet one summer and create a special community called "Goodsummer" where the "Friendly Four" play together and take care of one another.

*How the Guinea Fowl Got Her Spots: A Swahili Tale of Friendship* by Barbara Knutson (Carolrhoda Books, 1990) is a folktale about helping friends.

*Kids Against Bullying* <www.pacerkidsagainstbullying.org/> presents games and videos that can give children ideas for their own presentations about friendship and resolving conflict.

*The Little Red Hen Makes a Pizza* by Philemon Sturges (Dutton Children's Books, 1999) is a modern, hip retelling of the traditional tale of friends who won't help. An appealing choice for this age group that will get discussion started.

*Out on a Limb: A Guide to Getting Along* <http://www.urbanext.uiuc.edu/conflict/> is an interactive presentation from the University of Illinois Extension Department that asks children to decide on the course of action Maria should take in a situation of conflict. Text is printed and read aloud, making it a good choice for even struggling readers.

*Pirican Pic and Pirican Mor* by Hugh Lupton, illustrated by Yumi Heo (Barefoot Books, 2003), is an entertaining retelling of a Scottish folk tale about friendship and conflict.

*Tanuki's Gift: A Japanese Tale* by Tim Myers, illustrated by R. G. Roth (Marshall Cavendish, 2003), is a moving tale to spur discussion of the true value of friendship.

*True Friends: A Tale from Tanzania* by John Kilaka (House of Anansi Press, 2006) presents best friends, Rat and Elephant, and their struggle to save a friendship after fear, greed, and anger tear them apart.

**Hands On**

Use The Friendly Four to inspire kids to create their own version of a place called Goodsummer, with themselves as the main characters. Maps of Goodsummer and scenarios for friends to enjoy would provide a good basis for dramatic play and storytelling. Use True Friends and Tanuki's Gift to get children to make up their own traditional-type tales of friendship.

## Resource-Ready Core Collection

*39 Uses for a Friend* by Harriet Ziefert, illustrated by Rebecca Doughty (G. P. Putnam's, 2001), celebrates friendship in a funny, offbeat way.

*Alicia's Best Friends* by Lisa Jahn-Clough (Houghton Mifflin, 2003) examines the thorny problem of naming someone as your "best friend."

*Alien & Possum* series by Tony Johnson, illustrated by Tony DiTerlizzi (Simon & Schuster Books for Young Readers), is an easy reader.

*The Amazing Love Story of Mr. Morf* by Carll Cneut (Clarion Books, 2002) is about looking for friendship.

*Best Best Friends* by Margaret Chodos-Irvine (Harcourt, 2006) features children dealing with a jealousy-inspired argument and resolving the conflict themselves.

*Best Buds and others in the Adventures of Max and Pinky* series by Maxwell Eaton (Knopf) is an easy reader.

*Bob and Otto* by Robert O. Bruel, illustrated by Nick Bruel (Roaring Brook Press, 2007), tells the story of friends who develop different interests.

*Bud and Gabby* by Annie Davis (HarperCollins, 2006) discusses worrying about friends and qualities of friends.

*Clara and the Bossy* by Ruth Ohi (Annick Press, 2006) deals with the problem of bossiness.

*Cork & Fuzz and other in the series* by Dori Chaconas, illustrated by Lisa McCue (Viking), is an easy reader.

*A Couple of Boys Have the Best Week Ever* by Marla Frazee (Harcourt, 2008) presents two typical boys enjoying friendship, laughs, and not always doing what they are supposed to be doing.

*David's Drawings* by Cathryn Falwell (Lee & Low Books, 2001) shows how new kid David makes friends at a his new school.

*Days with Frog and Toad* by Arnold Lobel (HarperCollins, 1979) is an easy reader.

*Dealing with Secrets* by Don Middleton (PowerKids Press, 1999) looks at the good and bad aspects of secrets.

*Dog and Bear: Two Friends, Three Stories* by Laura Vaccaro Seeger (Roaring Brook Press, 2007) is an easy reader.

*Earth to Audrey* by Susan Hughes, illustrated by Stephane Poulin (Kids Can Press, 2005), presents friendship between a boy and girl who are very different from each other.

*Enemy Pie* by Derek Munson, illustrated by Tara Calahan King (Chronicle Books, 2000), tells how a boy bakes an enemy pie with his dad, only to find that the enemy has become his friend.

*Evie & Margie* by Bernard Waber (Houghton Mifflin, 2003) deals with jealousy between friends.

*A Friend for Dragon: Dragon's First Tale* by Dav Pilkey (Orchard Books, 1991) is an easy reader.

*From Me to You* by Anthony France, illustrated by Tiphanie Beeke (Candlewick Press, 2003), is about cheering up a friend.

*George and Martha: The Complete Stories about Two Best Friends* by James Marshall (Houghton Mifflin, 1997)

*Gossie & Gertie and others in the Gossie the Gosling and Friends* series by Olivier Dunrea (Houghton Mifflin) is an easy reader.

*Harry and Willy and Carrothead* by Judith Caseley (Greenwillow Books, 1991) talks about friendship and disability.

*Help! A Story of Friendship* by Holly Keller (Greenwillow Books, 2007) looks at gossip, friendship, and forgiveness.

*Herbie Jones Sails into Second Grade* and *Herbie Jones and the Second Grade Slippers* by Suzy Kline, illustrated by Sami Sweeten (Putnam's), are easy readers.

*Horace and Morris But Mostly Dolores* by James Howe, illustrated by Amy Walrod (Atheneum Books for Young Readers, 1999), deals well with inter-gender friendship and being your own person.

*How Humans Make Friends* by Loreen Leedy (Holiday House, 1996) offers a look at human friendship by an alien named Zork. A fun and non-preachy look at what friends do together, how they stay in touch, and how they solve problems.

*How to Be a Friend: A Guide to Making Friends and Keeping Them* by Laurene Krasny Brown and Marc Brown (Little, Brown, 1998) covers many practical topics such as dealing with shyness, addressing bullies, or resolving conflicts.

*Hunter's Best Friend at School* by Laura Malone Elliott, illustrations by Lynn Munsinger (HarperCollins, 2002), tells the story of a misbehaving friend and encourages readers to still be yourself.

*Iris and Walter* and others in the series by Elissa Haden Guest, illustrations by Christine Davenier (Harcourt), is an easy reader.

*The Lonely Moose* by John Segal (Hyperion Books for Children, 2007) looks at being a good friend.

*Making Friends* by Cassie Mayer (Heinemann Library, 2008) shows many different kids making friends and being good friends.

*Minnie and Moo* series by Denys Cazet (DK Publishing) is an easy reader.

*My Best Friend* by Mary Ann Rodman, illustrated by E. B. Lewis (Viking, 2005), examines the common childhood problem of trying to make friends with someone who thinks you are too young to be her friend.

*My Buddy, Slug* by Jarrett Krosoczka (Knopf, 2006) is an easy reader.

*My Friend is Sad* and others in the *Elephant and Piggie* series by Mo Willems (Hyperion Books for Children) is an easy reader.

*My Friend Isabelle* by Eliza Woloson, illustrated by Bryan Gough (Woodbine House, 2003), is an easy reader.

*My Friend Rabbit* by Eric Rohmann (Roaring Brook Press, 2002) is an easy reader.

*One of Those Days* by Amy Krouse Rosenthal, illustrated by Rebecca Doughty (Putnam's, 2006), shows that problems with friends are just one of many events that can make you feel glum, but tomorrow is always another day.

*Pearl and Wagner: Two Good Friends* by Kate McMullan, illustrated by R. W. Alley (Dial Books for Young Readers, 2003), is an easy reader.

*Pinky and Rex* series by James Howe, illustrated by Melissa Sweet (Aladdin Paperbacks) is an easy reader.

*Raymond and Nelda* by Barbara Bottner, illustrated by Nancy Hayashi (Peachtree, 2007), is an easy reader.

*The Remarkable Friendship of Mr. Cat and Mr. Rat* by Rick Walton, illustrated by Lisa McCue (Putnam's, 2006), looks at two creatures who first hate each other, then become friends.

*Riley and Rose* series by Jane Cutler, illustrated by Thomas F. Yezerski (Farrar, Straus & Giroux), is an easy reader.

*Simon and Molly Plus Hester* by Lisa Jahn-Clough (Houghton Mifflin, 2001) is an easy reader.

*Sylvie & True* by David McPhail (Farrar, Straus & Giroux, 2007) is an easy reader.

*That's What Friends Are For* by Valeri Gorbachev (Philomel, 2005) is an easy reader.

*Toot & Puddle* series by Holly Hobbie (Little, Brown) is an easy reader.

*Unlovable* by Dan Yaccarino (Holt, 2001) features a dog who is always teased but finally finds a friend.

*We Are Best Friends* by Aliki (Greenwillow, 1982) looks at how friends can still be friends after someone moves away.

*Wiggle and Waggle* by Caroline Arnold, illustrated by Mary Peterson (Charlesbridge, 2007), is an easy reader.

*Winnie & Ernst* series by Gina Freschet (Farrar, Straus & Giroux) is an easy reader.

*Wish, Change, Friend* by Ian Whybrow, illustrated by Tiphanie Beeke (M. K. McElderry, 2001), is an easy reader.

*Yes We Can!* by Sam McBratney, illustrations by Charles Fuge (HarperCollins, 2006) examines how to get along after teasing.

*Yo! Yes?* by Christopher Raschka (Orchard Books, 1993) is an easy reader.

## Resource-Ready Supplementary Collection

*Being a Leader* by Robin Nelson (Lerner, 2003)

*Friendliness* by Kristin Keller Thoennes (Capstone Press, 2005)

*Learning How to Be Kind* to Others by Susan Kent (PowerKids Press, 2001)

*Making Friends* by Sarah Levete (Stargazer Books, 2008)

*Manners at a Friend's Home* by Terri DeGezelle (Capstone Press, 2005)

*Moving* by Patricia J. Murphy (Heinemann Library, 2008)

*Respecting Others* by Robin Nelson (Lerner, 2003)

*Self-Respect* by Lucia Raatma (Bridgestone Books, 2002)

*Who Is a Friend* by Lisa Trumbauer (Yellow Umbrella Books, 2001)

## UNIT 3: *Outdoor Recreation in Our Community*
### (Grades 3 to 4)

## A Good Choice for Inquiry

Teachers and parents are concerned about the overuse of electronic games, computers, television, and other multimedia that keep kids indoors and physically inactive. This inquiry will help them to discover the opportunities that exist in the local community for healthy outdoor fun. Resources for this unit explore a wide variety of potential recreational activities, so there is something to suit every taste and ability.

Children who discover an activity that is of particular interest to them may want to focus on that activity alone. Others may want to create informative maps, posters, or brochures to explain recreational options to their peers. Projects could be organized by theme, by season, by age group—the possibilities are endless. Whatever the choice, children will discover what their own community has to offer. In the process, they may discover potential for new activities. These might require an organized campaign of letter writing or talking to local authorities. Through this, true inquiry is born.

Most school libraries have good collections on various sports, so the resource listings here focus on other outdoor activities such as camping and games. Children who choose a particular game or activity may need recourse to a subscription database.

## Background Reading

Teachers who are not outdoorsy may be reluctant to try outdoor activities with children. Background reading about the fun that children can have outdoors, and the benefits of leaving the gaming videos behind, may motivate teachers. Essential background reading should include pamphlets from local sports facilities and guides to your locality's parks and other outdoor amenities.

*Extreme Kids: How to Connect with Your Children through Today's Extreme (and Not So Extreme) Outdoor Sports* by Scott Graham (Wilderness Press, 2006) is written for parents, but teachers will find many ideas for potential outings.

*Great Big Book of Children's Games: Over 450 Indoor and Outdoor Games for Kids* by Debra Wise (McGraw-Hill, 2003) will provide teachers with ideas for easy outdoor games to try with their students.

## Unit Overview

An inquiry into community recreation is related to physical education but the learning outcomes are primarily in language arts. By the end of the inquiry, students will complete one of the following projects:

- present a promotional campaign for an outdoor recreational activity in their community
- present a guide to seasonal outdoor recreation in their community
- present a map, video, Web site, or other presentation format detailing outdoor recreational activities in their area
- present a report in any format making a clear argument for the establishment of a new outdoor recreational facility in their area, including the costs and benefits

## Guiding Questions

What makes an outdoor activity worthwhile? What activities do we have in our community? What activities could we have in our community?

## Specific Questions

- What do we do to have fun in our community?
- What are the different activities people do in our community?
- Do activities change with the season?
- What activities would people like to do that aren't available in our community?
- Could we make them available or are they impossible? What could we do instead?
- Do people travel to participate in activities they can't find in our community?
- Do people travel to our community for special activities?
- What kinds of activities do people do for fun?
- What kinds of activities take place outdoors?
- What kinds of activities take place indoors?
- What special equipment and training do we need for different recreational activities?
- How do we describe recreational activities? sports? pastimes? hobbies?
- Does our idea of fun change as we get older?
- What activities are most popular in our grades? with our parents? with older people?
- How much does each activity cost?
- Which activities are free?
- How far would you have to travel to take part in your favorite outdoor activity?

## Controlled Vocabulary

- Amusements
- Camping
- Games
- Outdoor recreation
- Play
- Recreation
- Sports
- For particular kinds of activities use Bird watching, Camping, Skateboarding.

## Internet-Friendly Phrases

■ "outdoor games"
■ "outdoor recreation"
■ "camping with kids"

## Kid-Friendly Categories

Google Directory >           Kids and Teens
*Search within*              Games > Outdoor and Yard Games
                             Health > Safety > Outdoor Safety
                             Sports and Hobbies

## Resources for *Outdoor Recreation in Our Community*

### *Raise Interest and Stimulate Discussion*

*101 Things You Gotta Do Before You're 12!* by Joanne O'Sullivan (Lark Books, 2007) may inspire kids to get new activities started in their community.

*The Months: Fun with Friends All Year 'Round!: A Poem* by Sara Coleridge (Lobster Press, 2007) is a reprint of her 1834 poem that will give children ideas for a seasonal book of their own.

*They Played What?!: The Weird History of Sports and Recreation* by Richard Platt (Two-Can, 2007) is an engaging and entertaining look at fairly common, fairly uncommon, and downright strange, forms of recreation.

### *Resource-Ready Core Collection*

*38 Ways to Entertain Your Parents on Summer Vacation* by Dette Hunter, illustrated by Kitty Macaulay (Annick Press, 2005), looks at fun activities that families pursue during summer vacation.

*The Anti-Boredom Book* edited by Marilyn Baille and Catherine Ripley (Owl Books, 2000) includes some unusual outdoor activities.

*Art, Culture & Entertainment* edited by John Haywood (Lorenz Books, 2001) explores the history of entertaining ourselves.

*Follow the Trail: A Young Person's Guide to the Great Outdoors* by Jessica Loy (Henry Holt, 2003) is full of information on preparing to enjoy the many outdoor activities available to campers.

*Girls and Their Horses: True Tales from American Girl* by Pleasant Company Publications (American Girl, 2000) will appeal to those involved in horse sports and to those who just wish they could.

*Go Outside!: Over 130 Activities for Outdoor Adventures* by Nancy Blakey, photographs by Dana Dean Doering (Tricycle Press, 2002), is divided into four seasonal chapters, with plenty of activities for both urban and rural communities.

*Kids Camp!: Activities for the Backyard or Wilderness* by Laurie M. Carlson and Judith Dammel (Chicago Review Press, 1995) offers lots of good advice to beginning campers, even if it is just to a backyard or local park.

*The Kids Campfire Book* by Jane Drake and Ann Love, illustrated by Heather Collins (Kids Can Press, 1998), will make kids want to head for the campfire for pit dinners and telling ghost stories in the great outdoors.

*Kids Gone Campin': The Young Camper's Guide to Having More Fun Outdoors* by Cherie Winner (Creative Publishing International, 2006) covers all the necessary preparations, plus how to set up camp and enjoy yourself in the outdoors.

*Play with Us: 100 Games from Around the World* by Oriol Ripoll (Chicago Review Press, 2002) groups games by type, giving rules for each and variations from around the world.

*Playing with Stuff: Outrageous Games with Ordinary Objects* by Ferry Piekart (Kane/ Miller Book Publishers, 2004) will surprise kids with the crazy games they can play outdoors with the simplest of household items.

*Recreation Director* by Kathleen Ermitage (Raintree Steck-Vaughn, 2000) is a topic not often covered by occupational series for children.

*Sporting Events: From Baseball to Skateboarding* by Gabriel Kaufman (Bearport Publishing, 2006) examines the history and possible future of many sports.

*Winter Day Play!: Activities, Crafts, and Games for Indoors and Out* by Nancy F. Castaldo (Chicago Review Press, 2001) explores ways to have fun when it snows.

## Resource-Ready Supplementary Collection

*Cheerleading* by Ursula Szwast (Heinemann Library, 2006)

*Fishing* (*Get Going! Hobbies* series) by Lisa Klobuchar (Heinemann Library, 2006)

*Hunting* (*Get Going! Hobbies* series) by Joan Lewis (Heinemann Library, 2006)

*Our Favorite Things to Do* by Lisa Trumbauer (Yellow Umbrella Books, 2001)

*Welcome to the World* series (Child's World, 2008)

**Reporting Our News**
*(Grades 5 to 6)*

## A Good Choice for Inquiry

Teachers are always looking for motivating ways to get students writing. Reporting offers a different approach to writing style than students may be used to. Students may never have met a real reporter and may think that newspapers are boring. Beginning with highly-motivating stories of student reporters and engaging narratives about real-life journalists will make this topic accessible to children. Interactive sites will help ease discomfort children may feel with the newspaper format by increasing their understanding of newspaper terminology and the way newspapers are put together.

There are many great stories that feature student reporters. Because of the great variety of reading levels and interest levels, they are appropriate for use with small self-selected literature circles. Students who like a light, humorous touch will find the story for them. Others who want to debate controversial issues will find that as well. Others still will find the adventure and real-life danger that can go with the job.

## Background Reading

Teachers who are broaching a newspaper project for the first time will be reassured by a few good professional resources and sample papers from real students.

*Kids in Print: Publishing a School Newspaper, 2nd Edition* by Mark Levin (Mind-Stretch Publishing, 2004), from the creator of NESPA (see below), contains helpful hints on getting organized and teaching the needed skills.

*NESPA: National Elementary Schools Press Association: Newspapers Online* <www.nespa. org/newspapers.html> presents examples for teachers to consider as models.

*ReadWriteThink: Lesson Plan: Creating a Classroom Newspaper* <www.readwritethink. org/lessons/lesson_view.asp?id=249> is one strategy for introducing the project.

*School Newspaper Advisor's Survival Guide* by Patricia Osborn (Jossey-Bass, 1998) is a good professional resource for both teacher and librarian.

## Unit Overview

An inquiry into reporting classroom or school news covers all areas of the national language arts standards. After this inquiry, students will:

■ present their contribution to a classroom newspaper
■ describe the challenges encountered in writing as a reporter

- describe other challenges related to reporting
- describe the role of classroom newspapers in a school
- describe the diversity of their audience
- assess the need for classroom newspapers in their school
- assess the cost and benefit of classroom newspapers in their school

## Guiding Questions

What news happens in our classroom and school? How do we report it? How could we report it?

## Specific Questions

- How do we find out what is happening in our community?
- What sources of news exist in our community?
- What is news?
- What does a reporter do?
- How do we find out about news in our school?
- What would be the best way to share news in our school?
- What are different ways to share news in our school?
- How do we communicate to other classes and to our parents about what our class is doing?
- How do you write news?
- Is news writing different from other writing?
- What ethical considerations need to be taken into account when you report the news?
- What costs will be involved in setting up a classroom newspaper?
- What fund-raising or other money-raising activities could support our newspaper?

## Controlled Vocabulary

- Journalists
- Newspaper publishing
- Newspapers
- For stories add Fiction

## Internet-Friendly Phrases

- "classroom newspaper"
- "school newspaper"
- "student newspapers"

## Kid-Friendly Categories

Google Directory >     Kids and Teens
*Search within*          News > Newspapers
                         School Time > English > Journalism

# Resources for *Reporting our News*

## *Raise Interest and Stimulate Discussion*

*Adam Canfield of The Slash* by Michael Winerip (Candlewick Press, 2005) is part of an engaging series featuring Adam and coeditor Jennifer of the feisty student monthly called The Slash. In this story, Adam discovers that the evil school principal is misusing school monies.

*Adam Canfield, Watch Your Back!* by Michael Winerip (Candlewick Press, 2007) explores themes of bullying, environmental issues, science fair scam, and racism in the second book in the series.

*Coyote School News* by Joan Sandin (H. Holt, 2003) is a school newspaper story set in 1938 Arizona.

*Dear Little Wolf* by Ian Whybrow, illustrated by Tony Ross (First Avenue Editions, 2000), is a humorous book in this British series that would make a good choice for reluctant readers who still enjoy silly stories featuring animal characters. Little Wolf works at a local weekly as a Dear Abby columnist named Mister Helpful.

*Ellen Fremedon: Journalist* by Joan Givner (Groundwood Books, 2005) is a Canadian story of two girls who publish a newspaper one summer and then find their stories are upsetting people.

*Geronimo Stilton* series (Scholastic) is a good choice for ELL and transitional readers who need the support of many illustrations.

*It Can't Be Done Nellie Bly!: A Reporter's Race Around the World* by Nancy Butcher (Peachtree, 2003) tells the story of this intrepid reporter's trip around the world in 1889.

*The Landry News: A Brand New School Story* by Andrew Clements (Simon & Schuster Books for Young Readers, 1999) stars another intrepid student reporter whose quest for truth gets her teacher in trouble.

*Meet the Gecko* by Wendelin Van Draanen, illustrated by Brian Biggs (Knopf, 2005), features the appealing geek named Nolan and his reporter dad trying to help TV superhero Chase Morton stop the sleazy tabloid reporter known as Mole.

*The Pen Is Mightier than the Sword* by Anne Mazer (Scholastic, 2001) features popular series character Abby Hayes as an advice columnist for the fifth-grade newspaper.

*Soccer Scoop* by Matt Christopher (Norwood House Press, 2008) stars a goalie named Mac Williams who is being ridiculed by the school's cartoonist.

*The Truth about Truman School* by Doni Hillestad Butler (Albert Whitman & Co., 2008) is a modern take on school newspaper stories, as two girls publish an alternative online newspaper that becomes prey to nasty gossip.

Use these resources for fiction and nonfiction small-group literature circles. This is an engaging and student-centered way to inspire interest in issues related to reporting. Kids who relate to young reporters in these books may get ideas for their own reporting projects.

## Resource-Ready Core Collection

*Extra Extra: The Who, What, Where, When and Why of Newspapers* by Linda Granfield, illustrated by Bill Slavin (Orchard Books, 1994), covers all the basics about how newspapers are put together.

*The Indian Lane Ink* <www.nespa.org/pdf/IndianLaneInkDec07.pdf>, <www.rtmsd.org/IndianLane/site/default.asp>, and <www.rtmsd.org/74752082621412957/blank/browse.asp?A=383&BMDRN=2000&BCOB=0&C=60496> are examples of this student newspaper.

*The Junior Seahawk Newsletter: The Oldest Continuously Published Elementary School Student Newspaper on the Internet!* <http://www.halcyon.com/arborhts/jrseahaw.html> is another example of a student newspaper online.

*Little Lancer Lightning* <http://www.ltsd.k12.pa.us/51082012592140560/site/default.asp?&5108Nav=|&NodeID=76> is an example of an online student newspaper.

*School Newspaper* by Rae Emmer (PowerKids Press, 2002) is a simple guide for students.

*wickED: Navigate the Newspaper* <www.tki.org.nz/r/wick_ed/literacy/newspaper.php> helps kids learn the vocabulary of newspaper layout.

*The Young Journalist's Book* [e-book] by Donna Guthrie (iBooks, 1998) is another guide for student newspaper production.

## Resource-Ready Supplementary Collection

*Broadcasting & Journalism (Female Firsts in Their Fields)* by Anne E. Hill (Chelsea House, 1999)

*The Daring Nellie Bly: America's Star Reporter* by Bonnie Christensen (Knopf, 2003)

*Demanding Justice: A Story about Mary Ann Shadd Cary* by Jeri Ferris, illustrations by Kimanne Smith (Carolrhoda, 2003)

*Katie Couric* by Erinn Banting (Weigl Publishers, 2008)

*Yours for Justice, Ida B. Wells* by Philip Dray, illustrated by Stephen Alcorn (Peachtree Publishers, 2008)

*Writing to Retell* by Jill Jarnow (PowerKids Press, 2006)

## Figure 5.1  Standards for Units 1-4

| **Language Arts** |
| --- |
| NL-ENG.K-12.1 Reading for Perspective |
| Students read…to acquire information. |
| NL-ENG.K-12.2 Understanding the Human Experience |
| Students read…to build an understanding of human experience. |
| NL-ENG.K-12.3 Evaluation Strategies |
| Students…draw on their prior experience, their interactions with other readers. |
| NL-ENG.K-12.4 Communication Skills |
| Students adjust their use of…language…to communicate effectively. |
| NL-ENG.K-12.5 Communication Strategies |
| Students…use different writing process elements appropriately. |
| NL-ENG.K-12.6 Applying Knowledge |
| Students apply knowledge of…media techniques…to discuss print and nonprint texts. |
| NL-ENG.K-12.7 Evaluating Data |
| Students conduct research…by generating idea and questions. They gather, evaluate, and synthesize data from a variety of sources (e.g., print and nonprint texts, artifacts, people) to communicate their discoveries in ways that suit their purpose and audience. |
| NL-ENG.K-12.8 Developing Research Skills |
| The choices people make have both present and future consequences. |
| NL-ENG.K-12.9 Multicultural Understanding |
| Students develop an understanding of and respect for diversity in language use. |
| NL-ENG.K-12.10 Applying Non-English Perspectives |
| Students whose first language is not English make use of their first language. |
| NL-ENG.K-12.11 Participating in Society |
| Students participate as knowledgeable, reflective, creative, and critical members of a variety of literacy communities. |
| NL-ENG.K-12.12 Applying Language Skills |
| Students use spoken, written, and visual language to accomplish their own purposes. |

# Chapter 6

# *Inquiry into Our Natural Environment*

## *Integrating Core Curriculum Content into Inquiry-Based Learning*

Providing a natural environment for our children to enjoy is a concern that parents and educators share. Part of the answer lies in educating our children to understand and appreciate the natural world around them and to ask practical questions about how we interact with nature in a way that is sustainable, ethical, and affordable. These units promote science as inquiry, the first learning goal of all science standards. Coupled with these scientific understandings are goals related to economics, geography, history, and civics.

Each unit incorporates science education and social science core curriculum standards that are central to each inquiry. The science education standards are based on national science education standards that have come from the National Academies of Science and the American Association for the Advancement of Science. These standards are listed in full on Education World®. All standards met by the units that follow are listed at the end of the chapter.

## UNIT 1: *From Seed to Plant to Table*
(PreK to K)

## A Good Choice for Inquiry

Growing food from scratch can be an immensely satisfying experience, especially when you get to eat the wonderfully fresh results of your labors. For children, a chance to get their hands dirty (whether in a small way inside the class or a big way in the schoolyard) gives this unit a special appeal. Planting seeds themselves gives the children real ownership of the inquiry and motivates them to watch the progress of the plants. Focusing on seeds provides lots of scope for comparison and hands-on sorting activities.

There are many, many books and other resources on this topic, especially for easy-to-grow and widely available seeds such as pumpkin, bean, and sunflower. Other plants such as apples can be investigated hands-on in class. During snack time and lunchtime, teachers will see children discussing the seeds in the fruit they have brought from home. Parents who enjoy gardening are good experts to have on board this project.

## Background Reading

Teachers don't have to be experienced gardeners to do this project. School gardens exist all over North America. Benefit from the advice of those who have already had success growing food plants with young children. A good reference text will help with any problems that arise, even if it is just to find an explanation rather than to solve the problem.

*The Edible Schoolyard* <www.edibleschoolyard.org> offers good how-to advice, resources, and tips for successfully starting a school garden.

*Gardening with Children* by Beth Richardson, photographs by Lynn Karlin (Taunton Press, 1998), describes how to involve children in gardening, from deciding what to plant to the moment of harvest.

*The Gardener's A-Z Guide to Growing Organic Food* by Tanya Denckla, illustrated by Stephen Alcorn (Storey Publishing, 2003) is a comprehensive, easy-to-follow manual.

## Unit Overview

An inquiry into how we grow the food we eat covers science goals related to scientific inquiry, life science, science and technology, personal and social perspectives, the history and nature of science, plus social science outcomes about our environment and society. By the end of this inquiry, children will:

- describe their plan to grow food
- describe the seeds they planted

- describe their observations of the growth of their garden
- predict what will happen to their garden after the unit is completed
- describe the life cycle of chosen plants

## Guiding Questions

How do we grow the food that we eat? What food could we grow?

## Specific Questions

- Where do seeds come from?
- What do seeds look like?
- How do seeds grow?
- Why are some plants big and others small?
- What do plants need to grow?
- What plants can't grow in our environment?
- What is the most common plant in our environment?
- How many different plants grow around our school?
- What plants are native to our environment? What plants have been brought here from other places?
- What is inside a seed?
- Do seeds need people to plant them? (How do seeds get into the ground without our help?)
- What is the difference between small family farms and huge factory farms?
- What does organic mean?
- What sizes do seeds come in?

## Controlled Vocabulary

- Ecology
- Gardening
- Gardens
- Plants
- Seeds
- Seeds dispersal
- Trees
- For particular kinds of seeds and plants use Apples, Pumpkin, Sunflowers.

## Internet-Friendly Phrases

- "growing pumpkins"
- "growing sunflowers"

# Kid-Friendly Categories

Google Directory >        Kids and Teens
*Search within*        Sports and Hobbies > Gardening
        School Time > Science > Farming

## Resources for *From Seed to Plant to Table*

### *Raise Interest and Stimulate Discussion*

*Apples: And How They Grow* by Laura Driscoll, illustrated by Tammy Smith (Grosset & Dunlap, 2003), is a good outline of the basics and covers specialized topics such as grafting.

*Busy in the Garden: Poems* by George Shannon, illustrated by Sam Williams (Greenwillow, 2006), contains rowdy and fun poems and riddles about growing vegetables that are sure to excite interest in young children.

*The Carrot Seed* by Ruth Krauss, illustrated by Crockett Johnson (HarperCollins, 1973), is a classic story about the patience required of a gardener.

*The Garden that We Grew* by Joan Holub, illustrations by Hiroe Nakata (Puffin Books, 2001), is an easy reader about growing pumpkins from seeds.

*A Grand Old Tree* by Mary Newell DePalma (A. A. Levine Books, 2005) follows the slow life cycle of a tree producing seeds. A good resource to inspire questions about seeds.

*How Are You Peeling? Foods with Moods* by Saxton Freymann and Joost Elffers (A. Levine, 1999) is a fun way to get kids identifying foods and discussing how they grow.

*How Many Seeds in a Pumpkin?* by Margaret McNamara, illustrated by G. Brian Karas (Schwartz & Wade Books, 2007), combines math and science concepts in a thoughtful story about self-perception.

*Pumpkin, Pumpkin* by Jeanne Titherington (Greenwillow Books, 1986) is the gentle story of a kid named Jack who plants a pumpkin and saves seeds to plant again in the spring.

*Pumpkin Town!: (or, Nothing is Better and Worse than Pumpkins)* by Katie McKay, illustrated by Pablo Bernasconi (Houghton Mifflin, 2006), is a tall tale that will have kids asking "Could it happen?"

*Seeds! Seeds! Seeds!* by Nancy Elizabeth Wallace (Marshall Cavendish, 2004) encourages children to start their own garden.

*Sunflower House* by Eve Bunting, illustrated by Kathryn Hewitt (Harcourt Brace, 1996), is another story about a boy who, having grown his own sunflower house, saves seeds to make another house next spring.

*Ten Seeds* by Ruth Brown (Alfred A. Knopf, 2001) is a counting book that looks at what can happen to seeds after they are planted.

*To Be Like the Sun* by Susan Marie Swanson, illustrated by Margaret Chodos-Irvine (Harcourt, 2008), is a child's reflection on how a tiny seed can become a sunflower.

*What Kinds of Seeds Are These?* by Heidi Roemer, illustrated by Olena Kassian (North Word, 2006), has inspiring paintings and rhyming riddles that cause children to question, "How do seeds get to where they will able to grow?"

*The Whole Green World* by Tony Johnston, illustrated by Elisa Kleven (Farrar, Straus & Giroux, 2005), is a well-illustrated rhyming ode to the joys of planting seeds.

**Hands On**

Use an idea from *Seeds! Seeds! Seeds!* to get children started on a garden. Prepare five bags as in the story and have them delivered to the class with a note from Buddy's grandpa.

## *Resource-Ready Core Collection*

*Beans* by Gail Saunders-Smith (Pebble Books, 1998) presents the life cycle of a bean in simple text.

*Big Red Apple* by Tony Johnson, illustrated by Judith Hoffman Corwin (Scholastic, 1999), shows how apple seeds get planted in nature.

*Bread Is for Eating* by David Gershator and Phillis Gershator, illustrated by Emma Shaw-Smith (Holt, 1998), tells the story of how bread begins with the planting of wheat seeds.

*Carrots* by Inez Snyder (Children's Press, 2004) follows a carrot from seed to when it is eaten.

*First Nature Activity Book* by Angela Wilkes (DK Publishing, 2007) includes collecting seeds from nature.

*From Bean to Bean Plant* by Anita Ganeri (Heinemann Library, 2006) presents the life cycle of a bean plant.

*From Seed to Apple* by Anita Ganeri (Heinemann Library, 2006) uses photographs, text, and drawings to explain the life cycle of an apple.

*From Seed to Plant* by Gail Gibbons (Holiday House, 1991) is a simple, clear presentation for young children.

*From Seed to Pumpkin* by Wendy Pfeffer, illustrated by James Graham Hale (HarperCollins, 2004), is written at a good level for preschool.

*From Seed to Sunflower* by Anita Ganeri (Heinemann Library, 2006) contains bold photographs and clear text.

*Fruit* by Lynn M. Stone (Rourke Publishing, 2008) is a well-written account of the importance of the seeds that fruit produce.

*A Fruit is a Suitcase for Seeds* by Jean Richards, illustrated by Anca Hariton (Millbrook Press, 2002), shows how these "suitcases" travel, allowing the seed to eventually grow.

*How a Seed Grows* by Helene J. Jordan, illustrated by Loretta Krupinski (HarperCollins, 1992), shows how children can plant bean seeds in eggshells and observe the plants grow.

*How Do Plants Grow?* by Louise Spilsbury and Richard Spilsbury (Heinemann, 2006) presents clearly labeled photographs to illustrate the science of plant growth.

*I Am an Apple* by Jean Marzollo, illustrated by Judith Moffatt (Scholastic, 1997), is an easy reader.

*I Am a Seed* by Jean Marzollo, illustrated by Judith Moffatt (Scholastic, 1996), is an easy reader.

*Pick, Pull, Snap!: Where Once a Flower Bloomed* by Lola M. Schaefer, illustrated by Lindsay Barrett George (Greenwillow Books, 2003), brilliantly illustrates the growth of foods from pollination to seed to fruit on gatefold flaps.

*Plant* by Penelope Arlon (DK Publishing, 2006) examines how plants grow from seeds and looks at edible plants.

*Plant Cycle* by Ray James (Rourke Publishing, 2007) is a simple text with excellent photographs.

*Plant Packages: A Book about Seeds* [e-book] by Susan Blackaby, illustrated by Charlene DeLage (Picture Window Books, 2003), is a good introduction to growing pumpkins from seeds.

*Plants Grow from Seeds* by Rachel Mann (Compass Point Books, 2004) is an easy reader that includes phonics instruction.

*The Pumpkin Book* by Gail Gibbons (Holiday House, 1999) includes instruction for drying seeds.

*Pumpkin Jack* by Will Hubbell (A. Whitman, 2000) shows that old pumpkins will seed themselves.

*A Seed in Need: A First Look at the Plant Cycle* by Sam Godwin, illustrated by Simone Abel (Picture Window Books, 2005), is a simple explanation of what seeds need to grow.

*Seeds* by Vijaya Bodach (Capstone Press, 2007) looks at the role of seeds in the life cycle of a plant and includes a discussion of the seeds that people eat.

*Seeds* by Ken Robbins (Atheneum Books for Young Readers, 2005) contains large, clear photographs and answers to many common questions, making this a perfect choice for preschoolers.

*Seeds* by Lynn M. Stone (Rourke Pub., 2008) is a well-written and clearly illustrated account of what happens to seeds as plants grow.

*Sunflower* by Jason Cooper (Rourke Pub., 2004) follows sunflowers from seed to harvest.

## Resource-Ready Supplementary Collection

*Carrots* by Gail Saunders-Smith (Pebble Books, 1998)

*Flowers, Fruits, and Seeds* by Angela Royston (Heinemann Library, 1999)

*From Seed to Plant* by Allan Fowler (Children's Press, 2001)

*From Seed to Sunflower* by Ian Smith (QED Publishing, 2004)

*Fruits* by Nicola Edwards (PowerKids Press, 2008)

*Fruits and Vegetables* by Carrie Branigan and Richard Dunne (Smart Apple Media, 2006)

*How Apple Trees Grow* by Joanne Mattern (Weekly Reader Early Learning Library, 2006)

*How Peas Grow* by Joanne Mattern (Weekly Reader Early Learning Library, 2006)

*How a Seed Grows into a Sunflower* by David Stewart, illustrated by Carolyn Franklin (Children's Press, 2008)

*Plant Life Cycles* by Anita Ganeri (Heinemann Library, 2005)

*Plants* by Peter D. Riley (Gareth Stevens Publishing, 2004)

*The Pumpkin Patch* by Elizabeth King (Puffin, 1990)

*Pumpkin Time* by Luana K. Mitten and Mary M. Wagner (Rourke Classroom Resources, 2004)

*Seeds* by Charlotte Guilain (Heinemann, 2008)

*Seeds* by Rachel Matthews (Chrysalis Education, 2006)

*Sunflowers* by Gail Saunders-Smith (Pebble Books, 1998)

*Why Do Plants Grow in Spring?* by Helen Orme (Gareth Stevens Publishing, 2004)

*Why Do Plants Have Flowers?* by Louise Spilsbury and Richard Spilsbury (Heinemann, 2006)

UNIT 1: *From Seed to Plant to Table*

## UNIT 2: Wild Birds in Our Environment
*(Grades 1 to 2)*

## A Good Choice for Inquiry

Loertscher's book entitled *Ban those Bird Units!* may have forever associated birds with bad pedagogy. While we all want to ban so-called "bird units" from the library program, we do not need to ban inquiry into birds. The first aspect of this unit that makes it a good candidate for inquiry is that all environments have birds. Whether students study local seabirds, songbirds, or street pigeons, there is plenty of scope for scientific observation, notation, and reporting on local populations of wild birds. This makes the topic concrete and ever-present in the real world of the child.

There are so many excellent books and other resources out there about birds. Once children get outdoors to explore or even just observe a feeder through a classroom window, they are likely to be bitten by the birding bug. As their knowledge of local birds grows, identifying and tracking what they see will help children to see themselves as young scientists. This is a topic of interest to every community member who believes that birds enrich the beauty of our local environment. Kids and teachers both will become more aware of their own natural environment and may develop a lifelong interest in observing local wild birds. Let's not dismiss birds. Instead, let's look at them afresh—the inquiry way.

## Background Reading

Teachers and librarians do not have to be experienced birders or even amateur nature watchers to become interested and confident about an inquiry into local wild birds. The scope for art and math integration alone will help convince teachers to pursue this topic. Becoming familiar with the following reference tools will help them feel at ease on excursions.

*All the Birds of North America* by Jack Griggs (Collins, 2002) is the American Bird Conservancy's field guide and an essential tool for bird watching.

*The American Bird Conservancy Guide to the 500 Most Important Bird Areas in the United States: Key Sites for Birds and Birding in all 50 States* by American Bird Conservancy (Random House, 2003) will help identify possible sites for field trips.

*Identify Yourself: The 50 Most Common Birding Identification Challenges* by Bill Thompson, illustrated by Julie Zickefoose (Houghton Mifflin, 2005), offers sensible advice to the uninitiated, including his "Top 20 Rules of the Bird Identification Game."

*The Nutty Birdwatcher* <www.birdnature.com/> covers everything from the basic survival needs of wild birds to seasonal migration charts by state.

## Unit Overview

An inquiry into wild birds covers science core content related to scientific inquiry, life science, personal and social perspectives, plus the history of nature and science. Social science goals include economics and geography. By the end of this inquiry, students will:

- identify a local wild bird
- describe the physical characteristics and behavior of a local wild bird
- describe the life cycle of a local wild bird
- describe the food needs of a local wild bird
- describe the cost of providing food for a local wild bird
- describe and mimic the call or song of a local wild bird
- describe the migration patterns of a local wild bird (if applicable)
- identify good habitats for finding their local wild bird
- present observations of a local wild bird
- describe how they kept track of their observations of a local wild bird

## Guiding Questions

What kinds of wild birds live in our locality? How do they live and interact with us? How can we make scientific observations of wild birds in our local environment?

## Specific Questions

- What are the relative sizes of birds in our environment?
- Do birds travel in different ways? How do they move? Can they run? Walk? Swim?
- What do they look like? How can we tell them apart?
- Why are the males different from the females?
- Do both parents help to raise the young?
- Do all birds sing?
- Can we learn to make bird calls?
- Will birds come if we make a good bird call?
- Can we get a whistle that would sound like a bird?
- Why can some birds talk like humans?
- How can birds survive in winter?
- Which birds are vegetarians?
- Do we have predatory birds?
- Which birds eat other creatures?
- Did birds evolve from dinosaurs?
- Can we attract birds to our school?
- Is it cruel to keep birds in cages?
- How do scientists know what they know about birds?
- How can scientists learn about migrating birds when they travel such vast distances?

■ What kinds of birds are there? How do we describe them? (By what they eat? Where they live?)

■ What is the difference between a wild bird and a domestic or pet bird?

## Controlled Vocabulary

■ Bill (Anatomy)
■ Birds
■ Bird watching
■ Birds migration
■ Birds habits and behaviors
■ Birds nests
■ Feathers
■ Wading birds
■ For particular kinds of birds use Eagles, Herons, Wading birds.

## Internet-Friendly Phrases

■ "bird watching"
■ "large birds"
■ "wading birds"

## Kid-Friendly Categories

Google Directory >       Kids and Teens
*Search within*          School Time > Science > Living Things > Animals > Birds
                         Sports and Hobbies > Birding

## Resources for *Wild Birds in Our Environment*

### *Raise Interest and Stimulate Discussion*

*All about Birds* [videorecording] (Schlessinger Media, 2006) gives an overview of physical characteristics and behavior. A comparison with reptiles and a visit to an aviary give this introductory appeal.

*Alphabet Birds* [e-book] by Philip A. Terzian (Bellingham Publishing, 2007) has clear photographs of birds in their natural environment, along with interesting (and sometimes amusing) information about the bird in a four-line rhyme. Project this e-book to stimulate postulation about the birds: Do they live in our environment? Are they wild? What clues do you see in the pictures that might tell you something about these birds?

*Animals in the Garden* by Elisabeth de Lambilly-Bresson (Gareth Stevens Publishing, 2007) will encourage children to talk about the birds they can observe outside the classroom and from home.

*Bird Log Kids: A Kid's Journal to Record Their Birding Experiences* by Deanna Brandt (Adventure Publications, 1998) is a good sample of how to keep a log—created for children between ages 5 and 12

*Birds* by Tracey Crawford (Heinemann Library, 2007) lists the general characteristics of birds, but none are identified, making this a good resource for asking, "Do we see any of these birds in our environment and can we identify them?"

*Birds Build Nests* by Yvonne Winer, illustrated by Tony Oliver (Charlesbridge, 2002), contains appealing photos and poetry to get kids talking.

*Blue Sky Bluebird* by Rick Chrustowski (Holt, 2004) has facts and artwork that are sure to inspire questions.

*The Boy Who Drew Birds: A Story of John James Audubon* by Jacqueline Davies, illustrated by Melissa Sweet (Houghton Mifflin, 2004), tells the fascinating story of how Audubon came up with the idea of tagging songbirds to find out if they returned to their nests after winter. Some of the crazy theories about what happened to songbirds in the winter may surprise children. This is an excellent resource to stimulate discussion and scientific curiosity in children.

*Counting Is for the Birds* by Frank Mazzola (Charlesbridge, 1997) provides unusual thumbnail sketches of some common North American birds: their favorite seeds and bugs, the temperament of the birds, and their enemies.

*Finding Birds in the Chesapeake Marsh: A Child's First Look* by Zora Aiken, illustrated by David Aiken (Tidewater Publishers, 2001), is a particular account of bird watching at a refuge that will help children plan their own bird-watching expeditions.

*Flute's Journey: The Life of a Wood Thrush* by Lynne Cherry (Harcourt Brace & Co., 1997) is a fictionalized narrative that engages children in the dangers faced by migratory birds, both from natural predators and from mankind's destruction of their habitat.

*Flying Giants (Dino World!)* [e-book] by Monica Hughes (Bearport, 2008) is simple enough for children to read themselves. Projected for the class to use together, it will encourage comparisons between ancient flying dinosaurs and modern-day birds. The illustrations will thrill dinosaur fans.

*A Poet's Bird Garden* by Laura Nyman Montenegro (Farrar, Straus & Giroux, 2007) focuses on what birds like and what makes an environment attractive to them.

*Tales Alive!: Bird Tales from Near & Far* by Susan Milord (Williamson Publishing, 1998) combines folktales from various cultures with scientific information related to birds. This is a resource that can be dipped into throughout an inquiry into birds.

*The True Story of Stellina* by Matteo Pericoli (Knopf, 2006) tells about caring for a bird in an urban environment.

*Watch Me Make a Bird Feeder* by Jack Otten (Children's Press, 2002) contains simple, clear instructions that may inspire children to build a feeder themselves so that they can observe particular kinds of birds.

Once students are ready to make observations of birds in the local environment, they may need the help of parents with digital photography and filming, especially those skilled at taking action shots. Children will have more success with binoculars than cameras.

## Resource-Ready Core Collection

*All about Birds: Bird Guide* <www.birds.cornell.edu/AllAboutBirds/BirdGuide/> is a comprehensive, clear guide to birds in North America. An easy-to-use resource, even for children, this collection offers everything kids will need to identify the range of the bird, the physical characteristics of males and females, nests and eggs, sounds and songs, and much more.

*Beaks* by Sneed B. Collard, illustrated by Robin Brickman (Charlesbridge, 2002), is a large format, kid-friendly volume that examines what and how birds use their beaks to eat. Simple sentences summing up the main idea and longer paragraphs with further detail make this resource useable by children of different reading abilities.

*Birds* [e-book] by Ann Heinrichs (Compass Point Books, 2003) uses stunning photographs and clear text that will give children information and ideas about how to observe birds in the wild.

*Birds* [e-book] by Ted O'Hare (Rourke Publishing, 2006) introduces many important concepts and vocabulary terms.

*Birds* by Adele Richardson (Capstone Press, 2005) is a good overview of the characteristics, eating habits, and reproduction of birds.

*Birds: A Close Up Look at Our Feathered Friends* (Look Closer series) by Sue Malyan (DK Publishing, 2005) discusses physical characteristics, habitat, and behavior that will help children make observations on field trips.

*Birds and Their Nests* by Linda Tagliaferro (Capstone Press, 2004) covers basic information about different birds and the types of nests they build.

*Birds in Summer* by Stephen Maslowski with Adele Richardson, photographs by Maslowski Wildlife Photography (Smart Apple Media, 2002), covers parenting, hatching, learning to fly and taking baths.

*Birds in the Fall* by Stephen Maslowski with Adele Richardson, photographs by Maslowski Wildlife Photography (Smart Apple Media, 2002), describes what birds need to migrate, how they prepare for migration, and the way they travel.

*Let's Look at Animal Feathers* by Wendy Perkins (Capstone Press, 2007) uses brief sentences paired with striking photographs to explain how feathers work, the different kinds of feathers, and why feathers are intriguing.

*Wading Birds* by Anne Welsbacher, photographs by John Netherton (Lerner, 1999), asks questions that will help children think about the physical appearance, behavior, and life cycle of this type of bird.

**Ask an Expert**

Ask children to report their observations to Cornell University through their "Classroom Feeder Watch" <www.birds.cornell.edu/AllAboutBirds/birding123/report/>. Students will learn more about scientific inquiry through direct contact with university scientists. Data they contribute becomes part of a North America-wide project to learn about bird populations.

## *Resource-Ready Supplementary Collection*

*About Birds: A Guide for Children* by Cathryn P. Sill, illustrated by John Sill (Peachtree Publishers, 1991)

*Baby Birds* by Helen Frost (Pebble Books, 1999)

*Beaks and Bills* by Mel Higginson (Rourke Publishing, 2007)

*Bird Eggs* by Helen Frost (Pebble Books, 1999)

*Bird Families* by Helen Frost (Pebble Books, 1999)

*Bird Nests* by Helen Frost (Pebble Books, 1999)

*Bird Watch* by Terry J. Jennings (QED Publishing, 2005)

*Birds* by Nicola Davies (Kingfisher, 2003)

*Birds* by Samantha Gray and Sarah Walker (DK Publishing, 2002)

*Birds (A First Look at Animals)* by Diane James and Sara Lynn, illustrated by Sue Cony (Two-Can Publishing, 2000)

*Birds* by Angela Wilkes, illustrated by Lisa Alderson (Kingfisher, 2002)

*Birds Build Nests* by Elaine Pascoe, photographs by Dwight Kuhn (Gareth Stevens, 2000)

*Birds of All Kinds* by Rebecca Sjonger and Bobbie Kalman (Crabtree Publishing, 2005)

*Birds of Prey* by Gerald Legg, illustrated by Bob Hersey (Franklin Watts, 2004)

*Birds Use Their Beaks* by Elaine Pascoe, photographs by Dwight Kuhn (Gareth Stevens, 2000)

*Cardinals* by Julie Murray (ABDO Publishing, 2002)

*Eagles: Birds of Prey* by Adele Richardson, illustrated by Linda Clavel (Bridgestone Books, 2002)

*Eggs* by Marilyn Singer, illustrated by Emma Stevenson (Holiday House, 2008)

*Feathers* by Cassie Mayer (Heinemann Library, 2006)

*From the Dinosaurs of the Past to the Birds of the Present* by Marianne Johnson (PowerKids, 2000)

*Gone Again Ptarmigan* by Jonathan London, illustrated by Jon Van Zyle (National Geographic Society, 2001)

*Great Bustard: The World's Heaviest Flying Bird* by Kirsten Hall (Bearport Publishing, 2007)

*The Hawk Family* by Bev Harvey (Chelsea Clubhouse Books, 2004)

*High, Higher, Highest: Animals That Go to Great Heights* by Michael Dahl, illustrated by Brian Jensen (Picture Window Books, 2006)

*Living Things in My Backyard* by Bobbie Kalman (Crabtree Publishing, 2008)

*Local Wildlife: What's in My Garden?* by Sally Hewitt (Stargazer Books, 2006)

*Loons* by Jill Katz (Smart Apple Media, 2003)

*Owls* by Julie Murray (ABDO Publishing, 2005)

*Owls Are Night Animals* by Joanne Mattern (Weekly Reader Learning Library, 2007)

*Owls: Flat-Faced Flyers* by Adele Richardson (Bridgestone Books, 2003)

*Puffins* by Helen Frost (Capstone Press, 2007)

*Red Knot: A Shorebird's Incredible Journey* by Nancy Carol Willis (Birdsong Books, 2006)

*Robins* by Jill Katz (Smart Apple Media, 2003)

*Saving the Whooping Crane* by Susan E. Goodman, illustrated by Phyllis V. Saroff (Millbrook Press, 2008)

*Today at the Bluebird Café: A Branchful of Birds* by Deborah Ruddell, illustrated by Joan Rankin (Margaret K. McElderry Books, 2007)

*Unbeatable Beaks* by Stephen R. Swinburne, illustrated by Joan Paley (Henry Holt, 1999)

*United Tweets of America: 50 State Birds: Their Stories, Their Glories* by Hudson Talbott (Putnam, 2008)

*Urban Roosts: Where Birds Nest in the City* by Barbara Bash (Sierra Club Books, 1990)

*Wading Birds: From Herons to Hammerkops* by Sara Swan Miller, illustrated by Jose Gonzales and Steven Savage (Franklin Watts, 2001)

*What Is a Bird?* by Lola M. Schaefer (Pebble Books, 2001)

*Whooping Crane* by Rob Theodorou, illustrated by Dewi Morris and Robert Sydenham (Heinemann Library, 2001)

*Why Am I a Bird?* by Greg Pyers (Raintree, 2006)

*Why Do Birds Sing?* by June Preszler (Capstone Press, 2007)

*Wildlife Gardens* by Lori Kinstad Pupeza (ABDO Publishing, 2002)

*Wings on the Wind: Bird Poems* collected and illustrated by Kate Kiesler (Clarion Books, 2002)

*Woodpeckers* by Jill Kalz (Smart Apple Media, 2003)

# UNIT 3: *Pests in Our Environment*
*(Grades 3 to 4)*

## A Good Choice for Inquiry

The endangered species unit is typical at these grades levels and the reasons for doing it laudable. However, most students cannot do hands-on investigation of endangered animals. Occasionally zoos and wildlife parks have programs to help boost numbers in the wild through breeding in captivity. For most students, visiting such sites is not possible, so an inquiry into endangered species is restricted to the use of secondary information sources. Resource-based inquiry makes better overall inquiry when there are hands-on activities for students and local experts to call upon.

Turned on its head, an inquiry into endangered species becomes an inquiry into pests. Every community has them. Urbanites love to share stories of rats in the sewers and cockroaches scuttling into dark corners. Wooden houses become prey to termites or raccoons. In rural areas (and even cities), larger animals such as bears and coyotes can be attracted to roadside garbage bags or dump sites. Killing insects that many people abhor is one thing, but when our fellow mammals join the hit list, people's opinions diverge. Some people even consider domestic animals pests. We are entering an area that is ripe for inquiry. Once you consider the problem and your own environment, even adults will discover that there is much they don't know about the pests in their own community.

Fortunately, there are many excellent resources to support this inquiry. Once students have focused on a particular type of pest to investigate, subscription databases will help to fill any gaps.

## Background Reading

*Ask the Bugman: Environmentally Safe Ways to Control Household Pests* by Richard Fagerlund and Johnna Lachnit, illustrations by Johnna Lachnit (University of New Mexico Press, 2002), is written for an adult audience, but its kid-friendly question-and-answer format makes it a good choice for reading aloud as well.

*Ball Identification Guide to Greenhouse Pests and Beneficials* by Stanton Gill and John Sanderson (Ball, 1998) contains photographs and descriptions of many pests, with photos of damage they can do and a guide to pest management.

*Tiny Game Hunting: Environmentally Healthy Ways to Trap and Kill the Pests in Your House and Garden* by Hilary Dole Klein and Adrian M. Wenner, illustrations by Courtlandt Johnson (University of California Press, 2001), provides hundreds of non-toxic options for dealing with pests.

Ask children to try out some of the traps at school. Based on the reading of *Don't Bug Me,* kids can invent their own pest-control logo and pamphlet explaining the nature of the pest, the damage it can cause, and how they deal with the pest in an environmentally-friendly way.

## Unit Overview

An inquiry into pests covers many science education standards related to scientific inquiry, life science, science and technology, and personal and social perspectives. Social science core content related to economics and geography are integrated as well. By the end of this inquiry, students will:

- identify a common pest in their environment and explain its physical characteristics and why it is considered a pest to humans
- present a plan for how it should be dealt with
- assess the economic costs and benefits of the plan
- explain the science and technology used to address this pest challenge
- explain the personal health implications of the pest eradication plan

## Guiding Questions

What pests live in our local environment and how should we deal with them?

## Specific Questions

- What do we mean when we say a creature is a pest?
- Are pests dangerous or just annoying?
- How do we deal with pests?
- What are the ethical implications of getting rid of pests?
- Are creatures considered pests in one environment but not in others?
- Does everyone agree on the definition of a pest?
- What pests can we identify in our environment?
- How should we deal with the pests in our environment?
- What costs are involved in dealing with pests?
- What financial damage can pests cause?
- Does everyone in our community agree on how we should deal with pests?
- What are the different viewpoints on pests in our community?
- Are plants ever pests? Are fish?

## Controlled Vocabulary

- Agricultural pests
- Agricultural pests control
- Garden pests
- Insect pests
- Insect pests control
- Insects as biological pest control agents
- Invasive species
- Pest control
- Pests
- For particular kinds of pests use Cockroaches, Mice, Rats, Zebra mussel.

## Internet-Friendly Phrases

- "agricultural pests"
- "garden pests"
- "household pests"
- "invasive species"
- "pest control"
- "squirrel control"

## Kid-Friendly Categories

Google Directory >      Kids and Teens
*Search within*       School Time > Science > Living Things

## Resources for *Pests in Our Environment*

### *Raise Interest and Stimulate Discussion*

*The Curse of the Were-Rabbit* [DVD Fiction] (DreamWorks Home Entertainment, 2005) stars the popular Wallace and Gromit, who start a humane pest-control business then find themselves up against a giant rabbit who is stealing produce for the Giant Vegetable Competition.

*Don't Bug Me* by Margo Sorenson, illustrated by Michael A. Aspengren (Perfection Learning, 1996), tells the story of Zach, who wants to teach his classmates a lesson after they tease him about his dad's pest control company.

### *Resource-Ready Core Collection*

*Cockroach* by Toney Allman (Kidhaven Press, 2004) looks at the insect's physical appearance, behavior, and habitat.

*Coyotes* [e-book] by Sandra Lee (Child's World, 2007) gives both sides of the issue on the question of whether or not coyotes are pests.

*Exotic Invaders: Killer Bees, Fire Ants, and Other Alien Species [Zebra Mussels, European Starlings, and African Honey Bees] are Infesting America!* by Jeanne M. Lesinski (Walker, 1996)

*Feeding the World* by Brenda Walpole (Sea-to-Sea, 2007) examines issues related to food supply, including pest control.

*From Pests to Pets: How Small Mammals Became Our Friends* by John Zeaman (Franklin Watts, 1998) examines our attitudes towards guinea pigs, rabbits, rats, mice, hamsters, gerbils, and ferrets.

*Grubs and Other Garden Pests* by Elaine Pascoe, photographs by Dwight Kuhn (Blackbirch Press, 2005), describes common garden pests and provides children with hands-on activities.

*Insect Wars* by Sara Van Dyck (Franklin Watts, 1997) takes a fascinating look at the raising of insects known as "beneficials," who are used by farmers and business owners to rid their environments of insect pests.

*Killer Bees* [e-book] by Meish Goldish (Bearport Publishing, 2008) describes the physical characteristics and life cycle of this dangerous insect. A map of its range in North America is included.

*Life in the Cities* by Sally Morgan, illustrations by Julie Carpenter, story by Pauline Lalor, story illustrations by Brent Linley (Two-Can, 2000), shows how pests survive even under harsh conditions.

*Oh, Rats!: The Story of Rats and People* by Albert Marrin, illustrated by C. B. Mordan (Dutton Children's Books, 2006), is an attractive and compelling read, giving answers to every question imaginable about rats, but especially about why they are such a "champion at survival."

*PestWorld for Kids* <http://www.pestworldforkids.org/home.asp> is a site developed by National Pest Management Association International. It covers 21 common household and yard pests. Children can test their knowledge with engaging, interactive quizzes and games, then use their knowledge "to outwit the world of pests."

*Unwelcome Guests* by Gary Miller (Chelsea House, 2005) takes a look at the destructive power of pests.

## Resource-Ready Supplementary Collection

*Beastly Bugs* by Lynn Huggins-Cooper (Smart Apple Media, 2007)

*Bugs Rule!* [e-book] by Kathryn Stevens (Child's World, 2008)

*Killer Bees* by Toney Allman (Kidhaven Press, 2004)

*Pests and Parasites* by Per Christiansen (Gareth Stevens Publishing, 2009)

*Poisonous Creatures* by Nathan Aaseng (Twenty-First Century Books, 1997)

*What Bit Me?* by D. M. Souza (Carolrhoda, 1991)

*The World's Most Dangerous Bugs* by Nick Healy (Capstone Press, 2006)

**UNIT 4:** *Extreme Weather in Our Environment*
*(Grades 5 to 6)*

## A Good Choice for Inquiry

Publishers of information books for children have recognized our growing obsession with climate change and the extreme weather events that are linked to global warming. There are many examples of recently published books on wild weather, storm chasers, and weather watchers. Combined with excellent informational Web sites and extensive archives of customizable raw data about weather, these resources contain a treasure trove of information to support inquiry.

Students are bombarded with news about the possible dire consequences of global warming. They may hear family and friends debating the issue. The topic of global warming, though widely reported, remains controversial. Conflicting claims and the complex nature of the issue make it a difficult subject for students to broach. Exploring extreme weather is a way to help children become informed about climate change with a subject that is more concrete, visually exciting, and locally relevant. There is hardly a community in North America without some experience of extreme weather, whether a catastrophic event such as Hurricane Katrina or more muted but still damaging events such as flooding, heavy snowfall, or high winds. Extreme weather events, studied from the experience and history of one's own community, is a motivating and thought-provoking topic for inquiry.

Extreme weather offers plenty of scope for extension activities. Students who want to move beyond their local community might choose to compare a weather event in their area to another, perhaps more extreme version, somewhere else. For instance, if their community has had a serious ice storm, they might want to compare it to the ice storm that hit Quebec and New England in 1998. This topic is well-suited to older students who are able to move inquiry beyond their own experience and environment to make connections to the wider world.

## Background Reading

Web sites listed in the resource-ready section can answer just about any question teachers and librarians might have about weather. However, teachers new to extreme weather concepts would do well to begin with Dan Satterfield's page aimed specifically at teachers.

*The Complete Idiot's Guide* makes a handy ready reference source and will appeal to some students once the unit is underway.

*The Complete Idiot's Guide to Extreme Weather* by Julie Bologna and Christopher Passante (Alpha, 2006) is a comprehensive resource explaining how weather systems create extreme conditions. A CD-ROM is included that contains hundreds of photos of storms and the damage they have caused.

*Dan's Wild Wild Weather Page for Teachers* <www.wildwildweather.com/teachers.htm> puts all the resources teachers need to brush up on their weather knowledge in one convenient place.

## Unit Overview

An inquiry into extreme weather covers many science education standards under physical science, earth science, science and technology, personal and social perspectives, and the history and nature of science. Social science outcomes related to civics, economics, and geography are covered as well. By the end of this inquiry, children will:

- present a report in any format that could be used to convince their community of the likelihood of a future extreme weather event
- provide a detailed plan to prepare their community for such an event, including the costs involved

## Guiding Questions

What kinds of extreme weather is our environment likely to have and how should our community prepare?

## Specific Questions

- What kinds of extreme weather is our environment likely to have?
- What causes extreme weather?
- Has weather gotten worse over the years?
- What records are available to tell us about the weather in our community in the past?
- How has our community prepared for the possibility of extreme weather?
- What is the financial cost of preparing for extreme weather?
- What kind of damage is likely to happen from extreme weather?
- What has damage from extreme weather cost us in the past?
- Are there other communities that experience similar extreme weather? How does our experience compare to theirs?
- How does climate change affect our weather?
- Is bad weather in our community connected to climate change?

## Controlled Vocabulary

- Climate change
- Meteorology
- Storms
- Weather
- For particular kinds of weather use Droughts, Dust storms, Ice storms, Tornados.
- For historical background add History

## Internet-Friendly Phrases

- "extreme weather"
- "climate change"
- "1998 ice storm" [or other specific weather event]

## Kid-Friendly Categories

Google Directory >        Kids and Teens
*Search From*        School Time > Science > The Earth > The Atmosphere choose:
                     Climate
                     Weather > Extreme Weather

## Resources for *Extreme Weather in Our Environment*

### *Raise Interest and Stimulate Discussion*

*The Man Who Named the Clouds* by Julie Hannah and Joan Holub, illustrations by Paige
     Billin-Frye (A. Whitman, 2006), combines biography with weather science. A child's
     monthly weather journal is included, which may inspire students to keep one.

*Records and Oddities (The Weather Report series)* by John Hopkins (Perfection Learning,
     2004) looks at strange facts related to hail, rain, wind, lightning, and temperature.

*Tornado Intercept* [videorecording] (National Geographic Society, 2006) follows a scientist and a
     filmmaker into the heart of a tornado in a special heavy vehicle with bulletproof glass.

*Weather Legends: Native American Lore and the Science of Weather* [e-book] by Carole
     Garbuny Vogel (Millbrook Press, 2001) presents a legend explaining a weather
     phenomenon, followed by a scientific explanation.

### *Resource-Ready Core Collection*

*Be a Storm Chaser* by David Louis Dreier (Gareth Stevens Publishing, 2008) uses Warren
     Faidley as the storm chaser consultant in this look at the science skills and
     knowledge that people in this profession use. The book includes descriptions of
     various kinds of extreme weather.

*Canadian Climate: National Climate Data and Information Archive* <www.climate.
     weatheroffice.ec.gc.ca/Welcome_e.html> allows students to generate customizable
     charts for locations across Canada. Extremes in weather are listed for the data interval
     chosen. Other pages on this Environment Canada site provide current weather warnings.

*Changing Weather: Storms* by Kelley MacAulay (Crabtree, 2006) explains the formation of
     various types of storms.

*Children's Weather Encyclopedia: Discover the Science behind Our Planet's Weather* by
     Louise Spilsbury (Parragon, 2007) is a large reference book covering weather systems.

*Chris Kridler's Sky Diary: Kidstorm* <http://skydiary.com/kids/> offers clearly written information about storms with engaging photographs that students may reproduce in projects if full credit is given. His links to important weather services is comprehensive.

*Dan's Wild Wild Weather Page* <www.wildwildweather.com> is written by Chief Meteorologist Dan Safferfield for kids interested in weather and forecasting. For students who cannot find a weather office in their community, this site provides a virtual tour of his forecast office.

*Earth's Weather and Climate* by Jim Pipe (Gareth Stevens Publishing, 2008) moves from everyday to extreme weather, recounting the work of "weather watchers."

*El Nino: Stormy Weather for People and Wildlife* by Caroline Arnold (Clarion Books, 1998) considers how marine life, birds, and mammals are affected for years after an extreme weather event. This book treats a complex subject in an accessible way for this age group.

*Extreme Weather* by John Farndon (DK Publishing, 2007) relates firsthand stories from people who have experienced extreme weather.

*Extreme Weather* by Terry J. Jennings (Smart Apple Media, 2005) includes a discussion of how meteorologists predict bad weather so that people can minimize damage.

*Extreme Weather: Science Tackles Global Warming and Climate Change* by Kathleen Simpson (National Geographic Children's Books, 2008) is a solid, up-to-date resource.

*National Climatic Data Center* <http://lwf.ncdc.noaa.gov/oa/land.html> is the world's largest archive of climate data. Follow the "Land Based" link to search for archival weather data. Students can create their own data summaries of extreme weather at county or state level, such as "Monthly Extremes." With records dating back to 1931, this is a powerful and versatile tool. Other data summaries support economic questions related to extreme weather, such as heating fuel demand. A special page is devoted to the economic and social benefits of NOAA <http://lwf.ncdc.noaa.gov/oa/esb/> with specific references to extreme events.

*Sunburns, Twisters, and Thunderclaps* by Janice Parker (Raintree Steck-Vaughn, 2000) explains how sun, wind, and water combine to create weather.

*U.S. Severe Weather Map: Weather Underground* <www.wunderground.com/severe.asp> clearly presents severe weather warnings on a map of America with county boundaries drawn. Links to other regions of the globe are provided.

*Weather* by Eduardo Banqueri (Enchanted Lion Books, 2006) is presented as a weather journal, including a lot of illustrations and photographic evidence.

*Wild Weather* by Caroline Harris and Warren Faidley (Kingfisher, 2005) uses astounding pictures and acetate overlays to show how storms are created.

*Wild Weather* by Monalisa Sengupta (PowerKids Press, 2008) looks at the origins and results of extreme weather.

## Resource-Ready Supplementary Collection

*100 Things You Should Know about Planet Earth* by Peter Riley (Mason Crest Publishers, 2003)

*1000 Things You Should Know about Planet Earth* by John Farndon (Mason Crest, 2003)

*The Atmosphere: Planetary Heat Engine* by Gregory Vogt (Twenty-First Century Books, 2007)

*Biomes of the Past and Future* (Earth's Changing Weather and Climate series) by Karen Donnelly (PowerKids Press, 2003)

*Blizzard!: The 1888 Whiteout* (X-treme Disasters that Changed America series) by Jacqueline A. Ball (Bearport, 2005)

*Changing Climate: Living with the Weather* by Louise Spilsbury (Raintree, 2006)

*Changing Climates* by Terry Jennings (Smart Apple Media, 2005)

*Cloud Cover* (Measuring the Weather series) by Alan Rodgers (Heinemann Library, 2007)

*Clouds* by Trudi Strain Trueit (Franklin Watts, 2002)

*Clouds, Rain, and Snow* (Weather Watcher's Library series) by Dean Galiano (Rosen Central, 2003)

*Coastlines* by Michael Kerrigan (Smart Apple Media, 2005)

*Drought and the Earth* (Science of Weather series) by Nikki Bundey (Carolrhoda, 2001)

*Drought and People* (Science of Weather series) by Nikki Bundey (Carolrhoda, 2001)

*Droughts of the Past and Future* by Karen J. Donnelly (PowerKids Press, 2003)

*The Earth's Weather* by Rebecca Harman (Heinemann Library, 2005)

*Earth's Wild Winds* by Sandra Friend (Twenty-First Century Books, 2002)

*El Nino & La Nina: Deadly Weather* by Carmen Bredeson (Enslow Publishers, 2002)

*Erosion* (Reading Essentials in Science series) by Virginia Castleman (Perfection Learning, 2004)

*Experiments with Weather* by Salvatore Tocci (Children's Press, 2003)

*Fire & Flood* by Sujatha Menon (PowerKids Press, 2008)

*Flooding and Drought* by Clive Gifford (Smart Apple Media, 2006)

*Floods of the Past and of the Future* (Earth's Changing Weather and Climate series) by Karen J. Donnelly (PowerKids Press, 2003)

*Forecast Earth: The Story of Climate Scientist Inez Fung* by Renee Skelton (Franklin Watts, 2005)

*Forecasting* by William F. Schley (Perfection Learning, 2004)

*Forecasting the Weather* by Alan Rodgers (Heinemann Library, 2007)

*Global Warming* by Neil Morris (World Almanac Library, 2007)

*Global Warming* by Chris Oxlade (Bridgestone Books, 2003)

*The Greenhouse Effect: Warming the Planet* by Darlene R. Stille (Compass Point Books, 2007)

*Hurricane & Tornado* by Jack Challoner (DK Publishing, 2004)

*Hurricanes* by Dean Galiano (Rosen Central, 2000)

*Hurricanes & Tornadoes* by Malini Sood (PowerKids Press, 2005)

*Hurricane Hunters & Tornado Chasers* by Gary Jeffrey, illustrated by Gianluca Garofalo (Rosen Central, 2008)

*Hurricanes, Typhoons, and Cyclones: Disaster & Survival* by Bonnie J. Ceban (Enslow Publishers, 2005)

*Ice Ages of the Past and the Future* by Karen J. Donnelly (PowerKids Press, 2003)

*Ice Storm!: The 1998 Freeze* by Bob Temple (Bearport, 2007)

*Inside Hurricanes and Tornadoes* by Neil Morris (Gareth Stevens Pub., 2007)

*Life in the Dust Bowl* by Sally Senzell Isaacs (Heinemann Library, 2002)

*Meteorology Projects with a Weather Station You Can Build* by Robert Gardner (Enslow Publishers, 2008)

*Natural Disasters* by John Hopkins (Perfection Learning, 2004)

*The New Book of El Nino* by Simon Beecroft, illustrated by Richard Rockwood and Rob Shone (Copper Beech Books, 1999)

*Rising Temperatures of the Past and the Future* by Karen J. Donnelly (PowerKids Press, 2003)

*Safety during Emergencies* by Lucia Raatma (Child's World, 2004)

*See-Through Storms* by Gill Paul, illustrated by Julian Baker and Janet Baker (Running Press Kids, 2006)

*Storm Chasers: On the Trail of Deadly Tornadoes* by Matt White (Capstone Curriculum Press, 2003)

*Storms and the Earth* by Nikki Bundey (Carolrhoda Books, 2001)

*Storms and People* by Nikki Bundey (Carolrhoda Books, 2001)

*Storms of the Past and the Future* by Karen J. Donnelly (PowerKids Press, 2003)

*Studying Weather* by Ted O'Hare (Rourke, 2003)

*Thunderstorms and Lightning* by Dean Galiano (Rosen Central, 2003)

*Tornado!: The Strongest Winds on Earth* by Mike Graf (Perfection Learning, 1999)

*Weather* by Brian Cosgrove (DK Publishing, 2007)

*Weather* by Bonnie Juettner (Kidhaven Press, 2004)

*Weather* by Susan Koehler (Rourke Publishing, 2008)

*Weather* by Randi Mehling (Chelsea House, 2007)

*Weather* by Chris Oxlade (Raintree Steck-Vaughn, 2001)

*Weather* by John Woodward (DK Publishing, 2007)

*Weather Maps* by Ian F. Mahaney (PowerKids Press, 2007)

*Weather Observation Satellites* by Allan B. Cobb (Rosen Central, 2003)

*Weather's Fury* [videorecording] (National Geographic Society, 2000)

*Weird Weather* by John Porell (Chelsea House, 2005)

*What's Up with the Weather?: A Look at Weather* by Traci Steckel Pedersen (Perfection Learning, 2006)

## Figure 6.1   Standards for Unit 1— *From Seed to Plant to Table*

| Science |
|---|
| NS.K-4.1 Science as Inquiry |
| Develop abilities necessary to do scientific inquiry. |
| Develop understandings about scientific inquiry. |
| NS.K-4.3 Life Science |
| Develop an understanding of the characteristics of organisms. |
| Develop an understanding of life cycles of organisms. |
| Develop an understanding of organisms and environments. |
| NS.K-4.5 Science and Technology |
| Develop understandings about science and technology. |
| NS.K-4.6 Personal and Social Perspectives |
| Develop understanding of types of resources. |
| Develop understanding of changes in environments. |
| Develop understanding of science and technology in local challenges. |
| NS.K-4.7 History and Nature of Science |
| Develop understanding of science as a human endeavor. |
| **Social Science** |
| NSS-EC.K-4.7 Markets |
| A price is what people pay when they buy a good or service. |
| NSS-G.K-12.1 The World in Spatial Terms |
| Understand how to use maps and other geographic representations. |
| NSS-G.K-12.5 Environment and Society |
| Understand how human actions modify the physical environment. |

## Figure 6.2 Standards for Unit 2— *Wild Birds in Our Environment*

| **Science** |
|---|
| NS.K-4.1 Science as Inquiry |
| Develop abilities necessary to do scientific inquiry. |
| Develop understandings about scientific inquiry. |
| NS.K-4.3 Life Science |
| Develop an understanding of the characteristics of organisms. |
| Develop an understanding of life cycles of organisms. |
| Develop an understanding of organisms and environments. |
| NS.K-4.5 Science and Technology |
| Develop understandings about science and technology. |
| NS.K-4.6 Personal and Social Perspectives |
| Develop understanding of types of resources. |
| Develop understanding of changes in environments. |
| Develop understanding of science and technology in local challenges. |
| NS.K-4.7 History and Nature of Science |
| Develop understanding of science as a human endeavor. |
| **Social Science** |
| NSS-EC.K-4.7 Markets |
| A price is what people pay when they buy a good or service. |
| NSS-G.K-12.1 The World in Spatial Terms |
| Understand how to use maps and other geographic representations. |
| NSS-G.K-12.5 Environment and Society |
| Understand how human actions modify the physical environment. |

## Figure 6.3 Standards for Unit 3— *Pests in Our Environment*

| Science |
|---|
| NS.K-4.1 Science as Inquiry |
| Develop abilities necessary to do scientific inquiry. |
| Develop understandings about scientific inquiry. |
| NS.K-4.3 Life Science |
| Develop an understanding of the characteristics of organisms. |
| Develop an understanding of the life cycle of organisms. |
| Develop an understanding of organisms and environments. |
| NS.K-4.5 Science and Technology |
| Develop understandings about science and technology. |
| NS.K-4.6 Personal and Social Perspectives |
| Develop understanding of personal health. |
| Develop understanding of types of resources. |
| Develop understanding of changes in environments. |
| Develop understanding of science and technology in local challenges. |

| Social Science |
|---|
| NSS-EC.K-4.1 Scarcity |
| People whose wants are satisfied by using goods and services are called consumers. |
| NSS-EC.K-4.7 Markets |
| A price is what people pay when they buy a good or service. |
| NSS-G.K-12.2 Places and regions |
| Understand the physical and human characteristics of places. |
| NSS-G.K-12.5 Environment and Society |
| Understand how human actions modify the physical environment. |
| Understand how physical systems affect human systems. |
| Understand the changes that occur in the…importance of resources. |

Figure 6.4 **Standards for Unit 4—**
*Extreme Weather in Our Environment*

| **Science** |
|---|
| NS.5-8.1 Science as Inquiry |
| Develop abilities necessary to do scientific inquiry. |
| Develop understandings about scientific inquiry. |
| NS.5-8.2 Physical Science |
| Develop an understanding of properties and changes of properties in matter. |
| Develop an understanding of motions and forces. |
| Develop an understanding of transfer of energy. |
| NS.5-8.4 Earth and Space Science |
| Develop an understanding of the structure of the earth system. |
| NS.5-8.5 Science and Technology |
| Develop understandings about science and technology. |
| NS.5-8.6 Science and Social Perspectives |
| Develop understanding of populations, resources, and environments. |
| Develop understanding of natural hazards. |
| Develop understanding of risks and benefits. |
| Develop understanding of science and technology in society. |
| NS.5-8.7 History and Nature of Science |
| Develop understanding of science as a human endeavor. |
| Develop understanding of the nature of science. |
| Develop understanding of the history of science. |
| **Social Science** |
| NSS-C.5-8.5 Roles of the Citizen |
| How can citizens take part in civic life? |
| NSS-EC.5-8.1 Scarcity |
| The choices people make have both present and future consequences. |
| NSS-G.K-12.1 The World in Spatial Terms |
| Understand how to use maps and other geographic representations. |
| NSS-G.K-12.5 Environment and Society |
| Understand how human actions modify the physical environment. |
| Understand how physical systems affect human systems. |
| Understand the changes that occur in the…importance of resources. |
| NSS-G.K-12.6 The Uses of Geography |
| Understand how to apply geography to interpret the past. |
| Understand how to apply geography to interpret the present and plan for the future. |

# Works Cited

American Association of School Librarians. *Standards for the 21st-Century Learner. 2007.* 7 Jan. 2008 <www.ala.org/ala/aasl/aaslproftools/learningstandards/AASL_Learning_Standards_2007.pdf>.

American College of Allergy, Asthma, and Immunology. *Medical Library: Children's Allergies. 2000.* 7 Oct. 2007 <http://www.medem.com/medlb/article_detaillb.cfm?article_ID=ZZZMBBWBSBC&sub_cat=255>.

American Library Association. *Information Literacy Standards for Student Learning: Standards and Indicators.* 1998. 7 Jan. 2008 <http://www.ala.org/ala/aasl/aaslproftools/informationpower/InformationLiteracyStandards_final.pdf>.

American Library Association. *Information Power: Building Partnerships for Learning.* Chicago: American Library Association, 1998.

Anderson, Lorin W., David R. Krathwohl, Peter W. Airasian, Kathleen A. Cruikshank, Richard E. Mayer, Paul. R. Pintrich, James Raths, and Merlin C. Wittrock. *A Taxonomoy for Learning, Teaching, and Assessing: A Revision of Bloom's Taxonomy of Educational Objectives.* New York: Longman, 2001.

Bevevino, Mary M., Joan Dengel, and Kenneth Adams. "Constructivist Theory in the Classroom: Internalizing Concepts through Inquiry Learning." The Clearing House 72 (1999): 275-279. Student Resource Center-Gold. Thomson Gale. 7 Oct. 2007 <www.galegroup.com>.

Bybee, R. W. *Piaget for Educators.* 2nd ed. Prospect Heights, Ill.: Waveland Press, 1990.

Callison, Daniel, and Leslie Preddy. *The Blue Book on Information Age Inquiry, Instruction, and Literacy.* Westport, CT: Libraries Unlimited, 2006.

Dewey, John. *The Child and the Curriculum.* Chicago: University of Chicago Press, 1902.

Dewey, John. *The School and Society and the Child and the Curriculum.* Chicago: The University of Chicago Press, 1990.

Donham, Jean. *"The Importance of the Model." Inquiry-Based Learning: Lessons from Library Power.* Worthington, OH: Linworth Publishing, 2001.

Education Development Center. *Youth Learn: Learning. 2003.* 7 Oct. 2007 <http://www.youthlearn.org/learning/activities/howto.asp>.

Education World. *Education World®: the Educator's Best Friends.* 2008. 7 Oct. 2007 <http://www.education-world.com/>.

Helm, Judy Harris, and Lillian Katz. Young Investigators: *The Project Approach in the Early Years.* New York: Teachers College Press, 2001.

Ikpeze, Chinwe H., and Fenice B. Boyd. *"Web-Based Inquiry Learning: Facilitating Thoughtful Literacy with WebQuests." The Reading Teacher* 60 (2007): 644-655. Student Resource Center-Gold. Thomson Gale. 7 Oct. 2007 <www.galegroup.com>.

Johnson, Doug. *"Designing Research Projects Students (and Teachers) Love."* MultiMedia Schools. Nov.-Dec. 1999. Doug Johnson: Writing, Speaking and Consulting on School Technology and Library Issues. 2007. 7 Oct. 2007 <http://dougjohnson.squarespace.com/ dougwri/designing-research-projects-students-and-teachers-love.html>.

Jorgenson, Olaf, and Rick Vanosdall. *"High-Stakes Testing: The Death of Science? What We Risk in Our Rush Toward Standardized Testing and the Three R's."* Phi Delta Kappan 83 (2002): 601. Student Resource Center-Gold. Thomson Gale. 7 Oct. 2007 <www.galegroup.com> [Also available at: <http://www.pdkintl.org/kappan/k0204jor.htm>].

Katz, Lillian G., and Sylvia C. Chard. *Engaging Children's Minds: The Project Approach.* Norwood, NJ: Ablex Publishing, 2000.

Kohn, Alfie. *Punished by Rewards: The Trouble with Gold Stars, Incentive Plans, A's, Praise, and Other Bribes.* Boston: Houghton Mifflin, 1993.

Krathwohl, David R. *"A Revision of Bloom's Taxonomy: An Overview."* Theory Into Practice 41 (2002): 212-218. Professional Development Collection. EBSCO. 18 May 2008 <http://search.ebscohost.com>.

Kuhlthau, Carol Collier. *"Inquiry-Based Learning." Inquiry-Based Learning: Lessons from Library Power.* Worthington, OH: Linworth Publishing, 2001.

Kuhlthau, Carol Collier, and Ross Todd. *"Guided Inquiry."* CISSL. 2007. 13 Jan. 2008. <http://cissl.scils.rutgers.edu/guided_inquiry/introduction.html>.

Loertscher, David V. *Ban Those Bird Units! 15 Models for Teaching and Learning in Information-rich and Technology-rich Environments.* Westport, CT: Libraries Unlimited, 2005.

McKenzie, Jamie. *"From Trivial Pursuit to Essential Questions and Standards-Based Learning." From Now On: The Educational Technology Journal* 10.5 (2001) <http://fno.org/feb01/pl.html>.

Mills, Heidi. *"The Dream." From the Ground Up: Creating a Culture of Inquiry.* Eds. Heidi Mills and Amy Donnelly. Portsmouth, NH: Heinemann, 2001.

National Research Council. *Eager to Learn: Educating Our Preschoolers.* Washington, DC: National Academy Press, 2001.

*No. 1 Cause of Injury in Elementary School: Playground Accidents.* Aug. 2007. 7 Oct. 2007 <http://www.usa.safekids.org/tier3_cd.cfm?folder_id=183&content_item_id=25113>.

Oberg, Diane. *"Teacher Transformation." Inquiry-Based Learning: Lessons from Library Power.* Worthington, OH: Linworth Publishing, 2001.

Oehlkers, William, and Heather Ruple. *"Inquiry into Action: A Model for Learning."* Reading Today. June-July 2007: 40-41. Student Resource Center-Gold. Thomson Gale. 7 Oct. 2007 <www.galegroup.com>.

Owens, Roxanne Farwick, Jennifer L. Hester, and William H. Teale. *"Where Do You Want to Go Today? Inquiry-Based Learning and Technology Integration: Providing a Choice of Subjects to Study and a Range of New Technologies with which to Study Them Produced Positive Results in Two Programs."* The Reading Teacher 55 (2002): 616-626. Student Resource Center-Gold. Thomson Gale. 7 Oct. 2007 <www.galegroup.com>.

*Partnership for 21st Century Skills. Framework for 21st Century Learning.* 2004. 7 Oct. 2007
    <www.21stcenturyskills.org/index.php?option=com_content&task=view&id=254&Itemi
    d=120>.

Pine, Jerome, and Pamela Aschbacher. *"Students' Learning of Inquiry in 'Inquiry' Curricula."* Phi
    Delta Kappan 88 (2006): 308-314. Student Resource Center-Gold. Thomson Gale. 7 Oct.
    2007 <www.galegroup.com>.

Serafini, Frank W. *"Dismantling the Factory Model of Assessment."* Reading & Writing Quarterly
    18 (2002):67-85, 2002.

Shamlin, Michele. *"Creating Curriculum with and for Children." From the Ground Up: Creating
    a Culture of Inquiry.* Eds. Heidi Mills and Amy Donnelly. Portsmouth, NH: Heinemann,
    2001.

Short, Kathy Gnagey, Jerome C. Harste, and Carolyn L. Burke. *Creating Classrooms for Authors
    and Inquirers.* 2nd ed. Portsmouth, NH: Heinemann, 1996.

Short, Kathy, and Carolyn L. Burke. *Curriculum as Inquiry.* n.d. 27 Jan. 2008
    <http://www.ed.arizona.edu/short/Publications/curriculum%20as%20inquiry.pdf>.

Sternberg, Robert J. *"Answering Questions and Questioning Answers: Guiding Children to
    Intellectual Excellence."* Phi Delta Kappan 76 (1994): 136-139. Student Resource Center-
    Gold. Thomson Gale. 30 Sep. 2007 <www.galegroup.com>.

*UIUC. About Inquiry.* 1998. 7 Oct. 2007 <http://www.exploratorium.edu/IFI/about/inquiry.html>.

Uno, Gordon E. *"Inquiry in the Classroom."* BioScience 40 (1990): 841-844. Student Resource
    Center-Gold. Thomson Gale. 7 Oct. 2007 <www.galegroup.com>.

Van Tassell, Mary Ann. *"Student Inquiry in Science: Asking Questions, Building Foundations, and
    Making Connections."* Action, Talk and Text: Learning and Teaching through Inquiry. Ed.
    Gordon Wells. New York: Teachers College Press, 2001.

Vanfossen, Phillip J, and James M. Shiveley. *"Things that Make You Go 'Hmmm...': Creating
    Inquiry 'Problems' in the Elementary Social Studies Classroom."* The Social Studies
    88 (1997): 71-78. Student Resource Center-Gold. Thomson Gale. 7 Oct. 2007 <www.
    galegroup.com>.

Wells, Gordon, ed. *Action, Talk and Text: Learning and Teaching through Inquiry.* New York:
    Teachers College Press, 2001.

Wilhelm, Jeff. *"Inquiry Starts Here: With Project-Based Lessons, You'll Deepen Kids' Learning
    Experience and Have More Fun Teaching."* Instructor. May-June 2007: 43-46. Student
    Resource Center-Gold. Thomson Gale. 30 Sep. 2007 <www.galegroup.com>.

# Index